Train Your Dog *Positively*

Train
Your Dog
Positively

Understand Your Dog and Solve Common
Behavior Problems Including Separation Anxiety,
Excessive Barking, Aggression, Housetraining,
Leash Pulling, and More!

VICTORIA STILWELL

TEN SPEED PRESS
Berkeley

Library of Congress Cataloging-in-Publication Data

Stilwell, Victoria.
 Train your dog positively : understand your dog and solve common behavior
problems including separation anxiety, excessive barking, aggression, housetraining, leash pulling, and more! / Victoria Stilwell.
    pages cm
 Includes bibliographical references and index.
 Summary: "Victoria Stilwell, positive reinforcement dog trainer and star of
the hit Animal Planet TV show, It's Me or the Dog, explains how to use her
force-free, scientifically-backed training methods to solve common canine
behavior problems"–Provided by publisher.
 1. Dogs–Training. 2. Dogs–Behavior. I. Title.
 SF431.S75 2013
 636.7'0835–dc23
                             2012045637

 Trade Paperback ISBN: 978-1-60774-414-6
 eBook ISBN: 978-1-60774-415-3

 Printed in the United States of America

 Design by Colleen Cain

 10 9 8 7 6

 First Edition

Contents

Acknowledgments

There are many people who have helped and inspired me to write this book. First among these is my husband, Van, who is such a remarkable man in every way: he has kept me sane through all the filming and traveling, and his editing has been instrumental in helping me to shape this book into what it is. He works tirelessly alongside me to spread the word about humane training and is dedicated to *positively* affecting the lives of dogs around the world. I also thank my beloved family on both sides of the pond for all their love and support, my dear friends who are always there for me, and my wonderful editor for this book, Lisa Westmoreland.

In my work as a dog trainer and author, I have been inspired by some of the greatest minds behind the science of modern dog training, including the incredible Dr. Patricia McConnell, Dr. Karen Pryor, Dr. Nicholas Dodman, Dr. Ian Dunbar, James O'Heare, Jean Donaldson, Dr. Stanley Coren, Suzanne Clothier, Pat Miller, Nicole Wilde, and more. Thank you to all those who have helped forge a path forward against sometimes stiff headwinds on behalf of the movement toward positive training.

Thanks also to my tremendous team of Victoria Stilwell Positively Dog Training (VSPDT) trainers. I am very proud to be affiliated with each of you and continue to be amazed and inspired by your passion, dedication, and drive to ensure that everyone has access to people who truly understand dogs and work hard to combat the damage that has been done by punitive training methods. Our shared goal of making the world a better place for dogs and their people is within reach!

To my father, Malcolm Stilwell, thank you for working so hard to give me the best start in life, and to my grandmother, Estelle Hepworth, for fostering my love of dogs. To Garry Gross, my former dog training partner in Manhattan, I loved sharing the journey with you. I miss you all so much.

And finally, I thank my daughter, Alexandra, who makes me a better person every day. Her goodness, kindness, compassion, sense of justice, and love for life, people, and animals is a constant inspiration and a joy to behold. I have been blessed with many fantastic opportunities and achievements in my career, but the production I am most proud of and honored to consider a success comes from being a wife and mother—raising a child who makes the world an infinitely better place. I am the proudest mother in the world, and I love you, Alex, with all my heart.

Introduction

"Positive reinforcement works great on easy dogs, but it's not really effective on severe aggression cases, is it?"

As one of the world's most vocal proponents of force-free dog training methods, I get asked this type of question frequently, usually by people who are pretty sure they already know the answer. Over the past several decades, science and history have taught us so much about how dogs think, feel, and learn, yet some dog trainers and owners still believe the only way to communicate effectively with a difficult dog is to "teach it who's boss" and force it into some mythical state called "calm submission." The issues arising from this common and fundamental misunderstanding of our canine companions are what motivate me every day to continue my work as a dog behavior consultant and educator.

There are many different terms used to describe the type of teaching methods I use: *positive reinforcement, reward-based, force-free,* and more. Proponents of these interrelated philosophies have a shared belief that it is much safer, more effective, and humane to teach animals using this overarching concept: If you reward a behavior you like, it is more likely that that behavior will be repeated. Similarly, if you ignore or redirect a behavior you don't like, it is more likely that incidences of that behavior will decrease.

That's a very simplistic synopsis of what reward-based training is and how it works, but that general concept lays the foundation for everything a dog owner needs to know to build a healthy relationship with any dog. Combine this concept with an awareness that dogs are not wolves trying to dominate us, so do not need to be controlled using dominance-based punishment techniques, and you have the recipe for what I call *positive training* throughout this book.*

Unfortunately (but predictably), those who still promote punitive, outdated traditional training methods aren't going quietly. There is a fierce debate raging in the dog training world between these two camps, and as a result, positive trainers regularly hear the same old tired arguments and accusations:

- There's more than one way to train a dog.
- Reward-based training methods don't work on severe behavior problems such as aggression.
- Dogs only "respect" leaders who assert their "dominance."
- Force-free trainers don't use discipline.
- Training a dog with food is tantamount to bribery.
- If you train a dog using food, he or she will respond only when you're holding treats.

---

* Note that use of the word *positive* in this case does not reflect the strict scientific description of the word as defined among the four quadrants of operant conditioning. For example, *positive punishment* is the addition of punishment during training, and I obviously do not condone or include such methods in my definition of the term *positive training* as I use it for the purposes of this book. Throughout this book, I refer to myself and others like me as *positive trainers*, and in doing so, I am referring to the same combination of reward-based training methods and non–dominance/punishment/alpha hierarchy awareness, not the scientific definition of the word.

- Dogs that misbehave or show aggression are trying to be dominant.

- Dogs are pack animals like wolves and are hell-bent on becoming the "alpha" or "top dog" over their owners.

Every one of these statements is almost completely backward, and I'll get to each one of them (and more) in detail in the course of this book. For now, I can say that there are many, many ways to effectively and humanely teach your dog—provided that you start from the basis of positive reinforcement principles rather than outdated and misguided theories of dog behavior.

There is a great deal of publicly available misinformation about how to build "balanced" relationships with our dogs based on "submission"—information that is purportedly the key to making our lives and relationships with our dogs better. If we could ask our dogs, I have no doubt they would let us know emphatically that such concepts as forced "balance" and supposedly contented "submission" are a pretty far cry from what they're actually feeling most of the time.

And that's one of the biggest problems in the dog training world today: those who promote what I call dominance, punitive, or compulsion training are realizing that the dog-owning public is figuring out that there must be a better, more effective and humane way to teach their dogs. As a result, these trainers have adapted and borrowed some of the science-based community's language, repackaged it, and are now selling it as their own marketing buzzwords: *Positive reinforcement. Reward-based. Gentle.* But no matter what they try to call it, traditional dominance and punishment trainers are using methods that are the exact opposite of the misappropriated labels they're using to sell their services.

There is a subset of hybrid trainers who actually do use positive reinforcement when teaching basic learning and language-building exercises but who either remain unconvinced that this training method will be effective or lack the confidence and skills to harness its power for more serious behavior problems. These trainers also employ punishment when dealing with "tougher" cases, even though these are the very dogs that would benefit the most from positive training and are most likely to regress further when punished or forced into so-called submissive states.

In truth, anyone can successfully employ positive reinforcement when teaching basic obedience and dealing with "easy" dogs, but it takes advanced knowledge, confidence, and strong leadership skills to successfully employ positive training on the most difficult behavioral cases. *What sets good positive trainers apart from punitive trainers is not just their ability to teach a dog to do* something *using force-free methods, but also how they manage to* stop *unwanted behaviors while still using humane training techniques instead of punishment.*

The landscape of the dog training world is now so confusing that owners who want a positive trainer have trouble figuring out exactly who fits that description. Compulsion trainers have seen their once-impregnable market shares start to shrink as trainers who follow modern behavioral science have begun to eat into their profits. TV shows like *It's Me or the Dog* and other media have made the public aware that there is indeed a better way to teach—*positively.* I've talked to people who told me they just didn't feel right using force and intimidation on their beloved canine companions, but the trainers they hired reassured them that they were using positive reinforcement. I can't blame people for falling for this clever marketing ploy—I've worked with dogs for a very long time, and sometimes even *I* still can't tell when someone actually believes what I believe or just knows enough buzzwords to squeak by.

This confusion and the difficulty people have trying to teach their dog humanely or to find a force-free trainer were the inspiration behind this book and the creation of Victoria Stilwell Positively Dog Training (VSPDT)—a global network of world-class professional positive reinforcement dog trainers united in their passion for promoting positive training in place of punishment and dominance. All VSPDT trainers have been individually assessed by me and verified to be practitioners of science-based, force-free methods. (For more information on sourcing a trainer, see the Resources section, page 225.)

As someone who is often referred to as a torchbearer of humane teaching methodologies, I struggle to understand how anyone can justify teaching a dog through the use of force and fear. While learning to become a dog trainer, I was taught all kinds of techniques that I've long since abandoned, and even though I never physically punished a dog, I found that even using aversives such as loud noises to interrupt or curb negative behavior just never *felt* right. The more I investigated the history and development of the science of dog behavior, the more certain I became that my instinctual doubts were justified and well-founded.

My love for and fascination with dogs has developed into a passion for making sure that people know there is a more effective, humane, rewarding, and enduring way to teach their dogs. This book will respond to many of the arguments you may hear from skeptics of positive training. It is designed to provide positive, humane solutions to some common (and often hard to live with) behaviors. Along the way, I'll also provide the scientific and anecdotal evidence to support why the scientific community and I can unequivocally state that trying to dominate a dog into what traditional trainers call "submission" through the use of force, punishment, and intimidation is inhumane, damaging, and ultimately less effective than science-based positive training.

The choice before any dog owner is a simple one: do you want your dog to follow you because she wants to or because she's scared of what will happen to her if she doesn't? To me, the answer is obvious.

PART ONE

THE RELATIONSHIP

The Way Dogs
Developed,
How They Learn,
and What We Need
to Know to
Understand Them

1

DOMINANCE AND PACK THEORY

Are Dogs on a Quest for World Domination?

Has anyone ever told you that if your dog goes through an open door ahead of you, it's a sign that he's asserting his dominance? Or if a dog walks in front of you or pulls on a leash, he is doing so because he wants to be pack leader? What about if he lies on a sofa, sleeps in your bed, or growls at you as you take his bone away? Are these really all signs of an intense struggle between man and dog over status in the household? Is everything a dog thinks, feels, and does the result of an unmitigated desire to dominate us, and everything else, in his quest to become top dog?

Concepts like these have been pounded into our public consciousness for decades, leading people to believe that any type of misbehavior by their dogs is a byproduct of an innate, instinctive desire to be dominant over everything and everyone—especially humans. This assumption forms the foundation of traditional dog training ideology, despite advances in modern behavioral science that I'll discuss later in the chapter. Indeed, much of the information still available to the general public promotes and endorses solutions to a dominance problem that doesn't really exist—at least not in the way some think it does.

Of course, that's not to say that there are no canine behavior problems to solve. My ever-growing workload as a dog trainer and behavior consultant attests to there being more problems than ever. What's more, they exist in large part precisely *because* this fundamental misunderstanding of dominance has been applied so broadly in our relationships with our dogs.

Most of the dog-owning public has long been misled into thinking that treating dominance is the key to solving most dog behavior problems, when the reality is quite different. Terms such as *alpha dog, top dog*, and *pack leader* have become part of our society's readily accepted and commonly understood lexicon. When these terms are used to describe *human* concepts of leadership and rank hierarchy, they can indeed be useful. But when we ascribe these concepts to our domesticated dogs, we are assuming, incorrectly, that dogs place the same value that we do on the practice of identifying who is of higher rank. Unfortunately, misunderstanding the source of a dog's behavior often results in unbalanced, unconfident, and ultimately unhappy dogs (and owners).

Think of dog training in medical terms. If you don't know what the root cause of a given problem is, you can't effectively treat it. Diagnosis and treatment can become skewed when too much emphasis is placed on symptoms rather than an investigation into root causes. And if you misdiagnose the disease, you usually end up applying the wrong treatment. In a best-case scenario, you've delayed the patient's recovery and will quickly realize the treatment isn't working, admit your mistake, and apply the correct remedy. In the worst case, an inappropriate treatment plan based on the misdiagnosis actually exacerbates the patient's condition, making it more difficult to solve, if and when you realize your mistake.

Unfortunately for dogs, a dominance-related misdiagnosis of their behavior problems usually leads to the worst-case scenario: traditionally prescribed behavior-modification techniques usually include punishment, intimidation, and fear—precisely the opposite of what dogs really need to overcome most behavioral issues.

If the result of this unfortunate process was merely unhappy, unfulfilled dogs, it would be incredibly sad but not an epic tragedy. But the problem is larger than that. The massive growth in dog ownership numbers, combined with this epidemic of punishment-based dog training, has created a population of dogs and dog owners who have never been more challenged to communicate effectively and safely. An increase in owner-surrendered pets at rescue shelters due to behavior problems has led to steadily increasing euthanasia rates. The number of dog bites and attacks, especially on children, are increasing despite local governments' attempts to approach the problem (from the wrong end of the leash) by using breed-specific legislation.

To find a more appropriate and hopeful solution, we need to appreciate how people came to so misunderstand and misdiagnose how our dogs think, feel, and learn. Then we will explore what modern behavioral science tells us is truly at play. We need to know how we got here and what needs to be changed so that we can more effectively, safely, and humanely build relationships with our dogs.

What Is Dominance?

To understand how the word *dominance* became so prevalent in describing dog-to-dog and human-to-dog social relationships, we have to look back at early studies of animal behavior. The term *pecking order* was originally used to explain the social hierarchies of domestic fowl in the 1920s.[1] Researchers observed that chickens commonly established what was assumed to be social rank by pecking at or threatening to peck each other. Since then, studies on social hierarchies have been done on many other species, and the evidence compiled from them has gradually helped us understand how animals form relationships and survive in social groups. Researchers conducting these later studies found that although dominant members of certain animal groups were more likely than others to display threatening or aggressive behavior if required, they would more often assert their influence (dominance) *without the use of force.* Other more submissive members of the animal group maintained the status quo by *offering* deference and appeasement behaviors to the more dominant members.[2] *In other words, dominance is not so much a character trait as it is a term that describes the relationship between animals, a relationship that is usually exerted without the use of force, thereby reducing the potential for conflict and ensuring safety and survival.*

This is a critical part of understanding how dogs interact. If a particular dog is dominant over another, such status is usually freely acknowledged and mutually understood—most often without issue. Misunderstanding the word and the role dominance plays in our dogs' lives has caused untold amounts of confusion. So I prefer to use the term *controlling behavior* when working with clients because it more accurately describes the domestic dog's social intentions.

Who's the Boss?

Traditional training theorists have led people to believe that social hierarchies among multidog households and human/dog families are *fixed*, with an "alpha" (dog or person) at the top of the hierarchy and other members of the human or canine family fitting nicely into slots underneath. Although social hierarchies do exist among dogs and certain dogs are more controlling than others, studies have shown that such dynamics are constantly changing.[3] Dogs that live in multidog households, for example, are usually able to work out among themselves who has primary access to what, depending on the value each dog places on a resource. For example, some dogs might place more value on a food resource when it comes to feeding time, whereas others may desire first choice for a preferred sleeping location. One dog usually does not control access to every single resource but will control those he deems to be of highest value to him. To maintain a safe and peaceful environment, a dog must be able to accept another dog's prior claim to certain resources.

Of course, as can be the case with humans, flare-ups of tension occur when dogs disagree over who has primary access to a certain resource. When two dogs place equal value on something (such as a bone, food bowl, toy, bed, potential mate, or even a human), they might fight because they are in direct competition over that resource, *not* because they are concerned about elevating their personal status within the hierarchy!

Although disagreements occur among dogs that have healthy relationships with each other, some dogs display socially inappropriate behavior, disrupting the status quo by bullying others. As with bullies generally, these dogs are usually quite the opposite of confident and self-assured.

Let's think about it in human terms for a moment. Is the common school bully the most confident kid in the class or the most insecure? Invariably, bullies are not confident people, and their need to control others by inflicting physical or emotional harm is driven by an acute insecurity rather than an abundance of healthy self-confidence. Canine bullies are also insecure, and although they may influence the behavior of other dogs, this is *still* not the result of a battle for rank. Macho, bullying behavior has no place in a natural, well-functioning dominant/submissive canine relationship or a human/canine relationship. Often, dogs that bully can best be described as having an acute case of bad manners or an unpleasant personality—just like humans. In the end, the sad fact is that there are some dogs that are, quite simply, jerks (although we still love them!).

We humans still find it very difficult to resist the idea that dogs share our interest in dominance and rank. Because we are capable of rational thought and intricate extrapolation of consequences, we may quest for ever-higher rank for many reasons: ego, desperation, revenge, boredom, insecurity, and ambition. Gaining high status demonstrates success in society and allows a person to have more control over others, earn a higher wage, and ensure future success. In contrast, dogs' perception of status is far less complex and emotional: if a dog values a certain resource or is more intent on achieving reproductive success than others are, he will notify those others that he is planning on protecting or controlling access to these things that make him feel good and ensure his safety and survival.

The great sadness in misunderstanding how dominance and submission work in healthy canine social relationships is that it has led to the use of training techniques designed to *force* a dog into a "submissive state." Those who employ forceful methods believe they are displaying leadership just like a "dominant" dog would do to establish rank; in reality they are behaving like socially inappropriate bullies. This in turn compromises a dog's ability to learn, and it significantly damages the bond between them.

So, to summarize, if "dominance" in the animal world means that force or violence is seldom used to maintain a functional status quo, why do some trainers and dog owners still believe that using forceful and punitive techniques to make their dogs submissive and establish themselves as the "pack leader" is the best way to teach them? They do so because the human concept of dominance (based on accumulating power, establishing higher rank, and exerting control in a forceful and sometimes violent way) muddles their understanding of canine relationships and social hierarchies and so dictates how they attempt to manage them.

Dogs Versus Wolves

So where did we go so wrong?

Dominance and pack theory in the dog world is based in large part on research collected from studies performed on a pack of unrelated, captive wolves in the 1970s. The results of these studies suggested that there was a *fixed* hierarchy in which "alphas" (leaders) had priority access to resources, *forcefully* maintaining the group structure through displays of aggression to others.[4]

Because dogs were descended from wolves, it was assumed that similar pack dynamics must exist among domestic dogs and that desire, drive, and competitive success would push "top dogs" to the top of the hierarachy. This theory became so popular that despite the obvious—that dogs and wolves are separated by thousands of years of evolution and that dogs and humans are completely different species—the theory was used to explain not only the social interactions between dogs but also how people should train them.

These captive-wolf studies have since been renounced by the very scientists who performed them and reached their original conclusions. It turns out that captive wolves with no choice but to live in unrelated groups (not their own blood-related families) behave very differently from members of what we now know to be a true natural wolf pack. Dr. David Mech, the wolf expert and senior scientist with the U.S. Geological Survey who was largely responsible for the original scientific study promoting "pack theory" (much of which he himself has since debunked), now explains that the behavioral differences between captive wolves like those used in his study and wolves in the wild are pronounced enough to call the results of his original research into question. According to modern behavioral science, any random group of undomesticated species artificially placed together will naturally compete with one another.[5] Scientific research has since concluded that in the wild, a true natural pack is actually composed of a mother and father and their offspring. This pack survives rather like a human family in which the parents take the leadership roles and the children follow. In a natural pack, harmony is created because, as we now know, deference behaviors are offered freely by the younger wolves rather than being forced onto them by their parents. This deference avoids injury that would compromise the pack's ability to hunt prey successfully.

The study's results were also skewed by the observation of subjects under severe stress because they were captives, forced to live with unrelated wolves in an unnatural environment, unable to behave as they would in a natural familial pack. These non-familial wolves had no choice but to interact with each other and develop coping mechanisms that caused them to become far more competitive and aggressive. And instead of focusing on the wolves' point of view, the researchers once again used their own *human interpretations* to conclude that the wolves were constantly driven by a desire to seek status over one another. Trouble is, no one really questioned at that point whether wolves really understood or shared our *human* concept of seeking status as a "rank reduction" process. It is more likely that for these captive wolves, the issue of rank was actually driven by something far simpler: the need for safety, survival, and reproductive success. Acquiring a resource safely would ensure survival, so although some wolves figured out how to hold onto their resources by challenging others and defending themselves, other wolves learned to ensure their survival by showing deference.

In short, Mech's researchers were observing a dysfunctional group of wolves using threat and deference displays to seek safety and survive within their unnatural captive group.

Unfortunately, the true nature of dominance, submission, and rank hierarchy has only recently been accurately understood. Because the results of those early behavioral studies were misinterpreted and misunderstood, dog trainers assumed that violent captive wolf behavior could be neatly transferred into a box labeled "dog behavior."

DOGS IN WOLVES' CLOTHING?

Even though dogs and wolves are genetically similar, they are separated by at least fifteen thousand years of domestication and that has changed them in many important ways. Today's domestic dog is approximately as genetically similar to the wolf as we humans are to chimpanzees. When you consider the evolutionary and behavioral chasm between chimps and ourselves, it becomes clear that although wolves and dogs share certain physiological and behavioral traits, they are far more different from each other than traditional pack theorists would have you believe. For example, dogs are one of the few types of animals who are willing and able to develop interspecies relationships. We take for granted how amazing dogs are, given their ability not only to tolerate but sometimes even befriend our pet cats, for example, while also developing close relationships with us humans. Not many animals (certainly not wolves) are able to bond with even one other species, let alone two or more.

Dogs are not socialized wolves. Not only has domestication set them apart physiologically, but it has greatly influenced their emotional development as well. The difference in developmental stages between wolves and dogs in early life is acute enough to affect their ability to form social relationships throughout their lives. For example, at just fourteen days old, wolf pups are able to walk around, eagerly investigating their environment, whereas canine puppies are still wobbly on their legs. Recent studies reveal that between the ages of four to eight weeks, canine puppies can successfully form interspecies social attachments in just ninety minutes.[6] Conversely, wolf pups could make the same social attachments only after twenty-four hours of constant contact with another species, and then only if all of the contact occurred before the pup was four weeks old. Although dogs generalize their social relationships to humans and are good at adapting to changing situations, wolves are very specific about their social attachments and do not adapt well to novelty, even when raised in captivity with or near humans. Interesting studies at the Department of Ethology at Eötvös Loránd University in Budapest demonstrated how aware canine puppies were to human body movement compared to wolf pups raised in the same domestic environment.[7] The puppies in this study showed an almost instinctive ability to follow the direction of a human point, whereas the wolf pups were disinterested and unable to make eye contact. The puppies naturally cooperated with the researchers and were much better at learning by observing and taking direction from them, whereas the domesticated wolves never looked to their human caregivers for guidance and behaved more as they would have in the wild, despite their domestication.

So if the captive wolf model led us down the wrong path, what model should we use to help us understand the dynamics of a modern dog pack? Observing feral dogs gives us a much more accurate picture of the domestic dog's social structure than either wild or captive wolf packs. It's more likely that modern domestic dogs are descended from solitary feral dogs that scavenged human garbage for food than from true familial packs. Although scavengers need a group for protection, they don't need a team to track and bring down prey and are usually more successful finding food when operating by themselves. In fact, having too many other dogs around means there is more competition for that food, resulting in a much looser social structure that changes with environment and situation—namely, with the abundance (or lack) of food. But thousands of years of separation from the wolf have also altered the social behavior of feral dogs: they don't stay in fixed family packs, and while the only wolves that mate in a pack are the breeding pair, mating is unrestricted in the feral dog population—it can occur among dogs within a family group or between dogs of different groups.

In conclusion, although their similar appearance and genetic proximity to one another make it tempting to assume that dogs and wolves behave the same way, they are dissimilar enough to warrant separate studies of their behavioral tendencies. When we don't understand these differences and misapply behavioral understandings from one to another, it can lead to gross misconceptions. Indeed, the most important distinction between dogs and wolves is that, while they are both animals with a primary natural instinct to be safe and survive, dogs and wolves learn in very different ways and place very different premiums on the value of interaction with other species.

Be the Pack Leader—Really?

Dogs are not wolves and they're not humans either. But it's a common refrain that is heard frequently among people in the dog world today: "Be the pack leader." Even people who aren't specifically talking about dogs or our relationships with them use this catchphrase regularly, and it has become a mainstay of human self-help and managerial doctrine. While it has value in a human-only scenario, it is dramatically misunderstood when applied to a dog's world.

As a species, humans are the most advanced, thoughtful, sentient beings in our planet's history. Not only do we feel emotions such as joy, jealousy, temptation, fear, and love, but we can also draw correlations between these emotions and the effect they have on our actions while also appreciating the impact our actions and words have on others. This is one of the most fundamental differences between humans and other beings (like dogs) that feel emotion—we care about what other people think of us. As far as we are aware, dogs don't have that ability. More precisely, the extent to which they care about what others think of them is limited to self-interest and well-being. For example, we may translate the joy our dogs display upon our return from a day at work as a signal of how much they love us and have hated the time they've spent apart from us (based on a long history of bonding and an unwavering expectation that they wouldn't be abandoned), but the dog may actually be feeling ecstatic elation that her provider of all good things (affection, food, companionship, and protection) has returned. It's not that dogs are selfish but they are egocentric.

Our ability to extrapolate, correlate, and sympathize has served us well as a species, but it has also created several unfortunate side effects that we sometimes have a hard time realizing are not shared by those around us—including dogs. We assume that because we suffer from varying degrees of overconfidence, and tend to be seduced by the accumulation of rank and power, dogs must do the same. Even dominance trainers often stress that you should never anthropomorphize (ascribe human characteristics to) your dog. I completely agree that we should resist the urge to "humanize" our dogs too much (while still recognizing that we share certain similarities). The irony is that to believe dogs see us as their pack leaders actually *requires* that we first anthropomorphize dogs by assuming they share our human concern regarding rank and what others think of us.

For example, my little Chihuahua-Terrier mix, Jasmine, doesn't care what my chocolate Labrador, Sadie, thinks of her when she slinks in to steal an antler that Sadie had been chewing. She's not worried about hurting Sadie's feelings. She just places a higher value on the antler at that moment and makes decisions that give her the best chance of getting it.

When we see our human intentions, motives, and responses in our dogs' behavior, we're effectively making things up as we go along; our dogs simply don't approach things the same way we do. Indeed, Jasmine may feel "envious" of Sadie for having the antler, but we must resist the urge to assume that Jasmine or Sadie really cares what the other thinks of her beyond how it will immediately affect her own individual well-being.

So because we now understand that dogs aren't in an ego-driven race to become the leader of the free world (or even just their own household), it follows that they also have no reason to suspect that that is our personal goal as well. Sure, they know that we are the ones who control access to food, water, and other things that allow them to survive and make them feel good, but we are also the ones who stop them from doing what they might otherwise naturally think is perfectly acceptable (chewing the sofa and peeing on the carpet come to mind). It is only when we misinterpret canine behavior that we start to think dogs must be trying to achieve a higher rank than us. And what's the highest possible rank? Pack leader, of course.

So the entire concept that we must assert our claim to the throne of pack leader before our dogs do is based on a mirage. For the sake of argument, though, let's say that dogs *are* completely motivated by a burning desire to become pack leader over their human counterparts. At some point in this theoretical exercise we must necessarily decide to disregard the simple truth—that dogs are well aware that we are not, in fact, dogs. Science gives us absolutely no reason to assume that because dogs have been domesticated so successfully that they can assimilate easily into our human world, they can somehow be fooled into thinking that we are not really humans at all but are strange, two-legged, hairless (for the most part) dogs. They know that we're not dogs just as well as we know they're not human. For some reason, though, dominance trainers like to emulate canine behavior by jabbing dogs with their fingertips, for example, pretending to "nip" as a mother dog does when she corrects her pups. These trainers believe that dogs make the association between jabbing fingers and the reprimands they once received from their canine mothers' mouths. I disagree. Dogs are much smarter than that!

To put the final nail in the coffin of the pack leader concept, however, we must return to this fact: true packs don't really exist in the domestic dog world in the first place. Putting aside briefly that dogs are not wolves and should not be treated as such, the definition of a true pack is, again, a mother, father, and their offspring—a combination usually found only in the wild (not in captivity). Very occasionally in wolf packs, a lone unrelated wolf may be "adopted" by an existing pack, but this is somewhat rare. Obviously, it is extremely rare to find a blood-related family of dogs—mother, father, and their offspring—living together as domestic pets in today's society. Therefore we should move away from calling our usually unrelated dogs living in one household a pack. I prefer to use the word *group* or *household*.

I'm not suggesting that dogs can't live well with each other in groups. Indeed, one of the primary benefits of their successful domestication is their adaptability and, arguably more important, their sociability. But animals live in packs precisely to ensure their survival—they rely on each other to help hunt and provide sustenance. Domestic dogs obviously do not (and at this point in their domestication usually *cannot*) rely on themselves to hunt, either individually or in groups—their survival and well-being are almost completely dependent on their relationships with us. So, although domestic dogs may not be pack animals, they *are* incredibly social animals able to develop relationships among themselves and several other species simultaneously, allowing them to live perfectly comfortably either as an "only dog" or as part of a multidog household.

It is time, therefore, to finally retire the term *pack leader*—especially when it refers to humans interacting with dogs. Domestic dogs don't live in true packs, and even if they did, we, as a different species, wouldn't be a part of them.

The Negative Impact of Dominance Theory on Dogs and People

"Dominance" has become the go-to diagnosis for all kinds of problem behaviors, such as pulling on the leash, jumping up, running through the door first, inappropriate elimination, destruction, barking, attention seeking, resource guarding, failure to respond to a command, and aggression toward animals, other dogs, family members, guests, and strangers.

To curb these behaviors, punitive trainers often suggest these tactics:

• Yank a dog harshly if he pulls.

• Stop a dog from pulling by using a choke, prong, or shock collar that will cause him pain if he tries.

- Knee a jumping dog in the chest.
- Keep a dog behind you when you go through a door.
- Rub a dog's nose in his excrement or urine to punish him for eliminating in the home.
- Put a spray or shock collar on a dog to curb barking.
- Ignore the dog completely whenever he demands affection.
- Punish a dog by jabbing him with your fingers (supposedly recreating the "nipping" of a wolf mother to her offspring).
- Kick or "nudge" a dog in the ribs to get his attention or to punish him for lunging.
- Restrain or "alpha roll" him onto his back or side if he aggresses.
- Keep a dog below you at all times, denying access to any high place such as the sofa or bed.

As I mentioned earlier, although dogs can be competitive and controlling toward people and other dogs (especially when there is a mutual desire for a valued resource), a dog is *not* demonstrating this socially inappropriate behavior because he wants to gain *status* over a person. This misunderstanding really frustrates me because it promotes confrontational relationships and validates the use of force and fear to train dogs in an effort to curb their supposed ascent. It's so sad watching people use choke chains, prong collars, and shock collars to yank, jerk, and shock their dogs into "behaving," yet no one thinks anything of it. Imagine if those same people taught children to behave using choke, prong, or shock collars. How quickly do you think they would (quite rightly) be called abusers?

Defenders of punishment-based methods in dog training are appalled when I dare equate teaching dogs with raising and teaching children. As a mother myself, I am well aware that dogs are not children—indeed, a massive part of my job is to convince owners not to anthropomorphize their dogs too much!

Modern behavioral science has shown us, however, that the dog's emotional brain is wired very much like a human's—dogs have emotions but not a human's level of complexity and ability to extrapolate. It is vital that people understand this, as it helps immeasurably to achieve the first step toward understanding our dogs: seeing the world from their point of view. Furthermore, studies have shown that the most socially mature dogs have an intelligence and ability to problem-solve and understand words and gestures similar to that of a two-year-old human child.[8] Dominance trainers might believe that dogs and children are completely different, but I'm sure even they would think twice about using aversives if they understood that dogs and toddlers have a similar level of understanding.

Culturally, we have gradually developed a nuanced approach to raising children that differs considerably from how we raised children even a few decades ago. Some may argue that modern views on how best to raise a confident, successful child are flawed overreactions to the more draconian, Victorian philosophies used by earlier generations—and to some extent, they may have a point. But I think most would agree we've made progress in understanding how children learn, and that far outweighs any potentially negative side effects of a newly "enlightened" approach: eschewing physical or emotional punishment of children for misdeeds or underperformance in favor of rewarding the good in our children and encouraging humble self-confidence.

As a mother, I am a wholehearted believer in celebrating the goodness of my daughter while gently and calmly redirecting any unwanted behaviors through the use of constructive guidance and discipline. I don't scream at my child or use physical punishment for misdeeds. And if her father and I need to address any negative behavior, we discuss the choices she made and implement consequences for those choices based on the situation.

In short, we are raising our daughter using all the same positive reinforcement philosophies that I use in my dog training. We've made great strides in how we raise our children; now it's time we do the same with our dogs.

Children and dogs are vulnerable beings that depend on their family unit to keep them safe, provide for them, give them confidence, and help them learn. The better we do as parents to help our children grow, the more successful they will be as adults. Being a good parent is a learning process, and it can sometimes be hard to negotiate challenges that are put in our path. Determining how we discipline our children is as crucial as how we encourage them to learn and experience life. As "pet parents" we face the same challenges when raising our dogs. The problem is, sometimes raising our dogs successfully can be even harder, because they don't speak our language and we regularly misinterpret theirs. So we latch onto any information out there that seems to have the potential to help us, and if we are unfortunate enough to watch the wrong television show, read the wrong book, or meet the wrong trainer, we will learn that teaching a dog through force and fear is okay. These trainers won't be called abusers for training dogs harshly, even though a dog is just as vulnerable and confused as a small child is without guidance. Unfortunately, a common mind-set remains that dogs are just dogs and we can do whatever we like with them to show our dominance and ensure that we establish ourselves as leaders of the pack, even if that means we hurt them physically or mentally in the process.

The Dangers of Punishment

Decoding the dominance myth is the first step toward creating a truly balanced and healthy relationship with our dogs. But diminishing the concept of dominance and hierarchy does more than just make our teaching more effective—it also keeps us safer.

Attempting to establish dominance over your dog can be very dangerous. There has been a dramatic rise in the number of reported dog bites in recent years, and although there are many reasons for this, I believe confrontational dominance training methods have played a large role. A study published in the *Journal of Applied Animal Behavior* concludes that confrontational training methods practiced by many trainers and handlers are a contributing factor to increased incidences of dog bites. This scientific study found that many confrontational training methods, such as hitting dogs, intimidating them with punitive force, and using techniques of restraint like the "alpha roll," did little to correct improper behavior and actually increased the likelihood of aggressive responses.[9]

Behavior is closely linked to and influenced by emotions, so punishing a dog for not obeying a command or for unwanted behavior while not understanding why the behavior is happening (and what emotional effect it is having on the dog) only serves to make the behavior worse. Punishments such as leash jerks and collar corrections, hitting, poking, "nudging," kicking, hanging by the collar, or using electric shock or spray collars may be effective in suppressing behavior at that moment, but these techniques do little to solve the problem in the long term and can make a dog's behavior much worse in the future.

One popular punishment technique used by dominance trainers is the so-called "alpha roll," in which the dog is restrained on his back or side until he "calms down." It may indeed appear that the dog has become quiet and relaxed, but he has actually employed an instinctive survival tool we call "shut down." This response is used by animals to appease aggressors and avoid any further violence. If the dog remains still or "shuts down" until the aggressor moves away, he is more likely to be safe. Even if a restrained dog's demeanor appears calm on the outside, research has proven that forced submission or restraint raises a dog's stress levels, due to a release of cortisol into the dog's bloodstream. Cortisol is a hormone that is produced in the adrenal gland and released in response to stress. Elevated stress inhibits learning and compromises a dog's ability to function normally. To the untrained eye, a restrained dog's stillness may indicate that he is calm, but in reality he is fighting an internal battle of survival as he tries to cope with what is, in essence, a stressful episode brought on by of an act of physical violence by a human, in which he is the victim.[10] Any "success" that may be achieved when using dominance techniques on even a mildly aggressive dog is generally just a case of the dog's "shutting down," suppressing his true instincts and valuable warning signals. Trying to "put the dog in his place" usually results in a short-lived quick fix, merely postponing the inevitable negative response once the dog feels threatened again. This delayed reaction can easily resurface at the worst possible moment, such as around children or in public.

A dog that signals his discomfort is much less dangerous than a dog that has learned to suppress his threat displays because of punishment and therefore does not give a warning before he bites. As a trainer who regularly works with aggressive dogs, I rely on such warning signals to keep me safe, so techniques that result in the suppression of threat displays and that fail to identify and treat the root of the problem create dogs that are very dangerous. People who use these techniques are at great risk: they may be bitten or their dogs may bite someone else.

The tragedy of dominance training techniques is that owners are learning these methods without realizing that they are making their dogs more unpredictable and dangerous. Although punishment may bring temporary relief for a frustrated dog owner's anger, it damages the human-animal bond and leads to mistrust, pain, fear, agitation, and increasing anger as the dog develops a strong negative association with the punisher. Far from treating the underlying motivation of the behavior, punishment almost always increases the dog's insecurity while decreasing his ability to learn.

*Ultimately, punishment-based techniques emphasize **what not to do** instead of helping a dog learn and understand **what to do**.*

I have seen countless trainers give appalling advice to their clients, for example, telling children (yes, children!) to reprimand their dogs by yanking their collars or hitting them in the chest or on the nose. I have seen people get bitten when told to groom their dogs no matter how much those dogs growled and showed their teeth, just so they could establish themselves as "alpha." I have seen a trainer wrestle with a muzzled aggressive dog until it finally submitted and then heard him declare that the "training" had been a success and the dog rehabilitated, even though he was still wearing his muzzle and cowering in the corner.

Think about how you learn. When you're emotional, it's difficult to think rationally and clearly because your "thinking" brain shuts down. Once you calm down, your body activates the "thinking" part of your brain again so that you can listen, digest, and learn, which in turn deactivates your emotional brain. The same principles are in play with our dogs. When we treat an aggressive dog with more aggression, not only do we compromise that dog's ability to learn, but the lasting results from our punitive treatment can range from disappointing to disastrous.

I feel very sorry for dogs that have been taught using punitive techniques and have met too many that have been subjected to a "professional" rough hand and are suffering behavioral issues as a result. I am not saying that punitive training techniques won't stop a dog's negative behavior at that moment. They often do, and the results can sometimes be achieved very quickly, but at what cost to your dog and at what cost to you? And how long will those results last? Anyone can make a dog do anything through force and claim the "successful" result as an impressive achievement, but there is nothing heroic, commendable, or reliable about dominating any animal into compliance. The beauty of positive training is that you can build a strong bond with your dog and teach compliance at the same time: the perfect recipe for a successful and fulfilling relationship.

2

THE POWER OF
POSITIVE TRAINING

So the outdated dominance and punishment-based theories behind traditional training techniques are flawed. Where does that leave us? Knowing where dogs come from, what drives them, and how they learn makes it clear that the most humane, effective, and long-lasting training methods employ the power of positive reinforcement.

Throughout this book, I'll be relying on your understanding of the concept of positive reinforcement as we walk through how to overcome and prevent behavior problems, so it's important at this point to again clearly define what the term means (and what it does *not* mean). *Positive reinforcement* can go by many names, all of which are valid: *reward-based training*, *science-based training*, *force-free* or *pain-free training*, and so on. Regardless of the terminology, the general theory behind this way of thinking remains the same.

So what exactly is positive reinforcement? Basically, it's simply this: Your dog learns that good things happen to her when she does the thing you like. If you give your dog a reward (praise, play, food, toys) when she responds to you or offers an action or a behavior that you like, then that behavior is likely to be repeated.

Positive-reinforcement teaching techniques use nonconfrontational methods to work a dog's brain:

- rewarding positive behavior
- establishing rituals and training actions that are incompatible with negative behavior
- lessening a dog's anger and frustration

And these methods can all be used while enabling the dog to feel good inside. If you reinforce your dog's desirable behaviors, there is less chance that she will indulge in other behaviors you don't like. If her decision making is influenced without the use of force, her trust in you is not violated.

Using positive techniques to change undesirable behavior requires that you first determine the cause of the behavior and then figure out how to modify and change it by giving your dog the ability to learn and feel differently. Owners who use these techniques learn to connect with their dogs and work through problems in a humane manner—strengthening the relationship by fostering mutual trust, providing affection, and encouraging cooperation. Increasing a dog's enjoyment of social interaction gives the dog what she needs to deal with the pressures of domestic life. Dogs that are taught using positive reinforcement methods are more tolerant and self-controlled and behave much more predictably in different situations.

It is vitally important for me as a dog trainer to help owners learn how to give their dogs the things they need to live successfully in our strange human world. A dog that is given consistent guidance from an early age grows up to be a confident dog. Guidance brings security, security brings confidence, and a confident dog has no need to show anxiety-based behaviors.

Positive Not *Permissive*

Most positive trainers do use discipline in the form of vocal interrupters, time-outs, ignoring negative behavior, or removing something that the dog wants, all of which are meant to guide the dog into making the right choices rather than force her to behave out of fear. In technical terms, such discipline is called *negative punishment* because it *removes* (*negative* = *minus, less*) something that the dog likes, such as your attention, access to you, or a favorite toy. This is by no means to be confused with the term *positive punishment*, which, though it includes the word *positive*, is defined as punishing the dog by *adding* something to the equation that the dog does *not* like (harsh corrections, physical force, intimidation).

Positive training is a much safer method for teaching aggressive dogs because it changes the way these dogs react by showing them that they can feel differently about a particular situation, thereby reducing or eliminating their need to aggress. Using these techniques allows owners to be proactive rather than reactive and puts the emphasis on teaching their dog what to do in a certain situation rather than on punishment.

The strongest relationships between dogs and humans are based on cooperation and kindness rather than on human dominance and animal submission. Choosing to use positive techniques when building a relationship with your dog puts you well on your way to establishing and maintaining increased trust and a stronger, healthier bond between you and your dog. Put simply, if your dog feels good about you, she will be happier, confident, better behaved, and more inclined to respond to you when you ask her to do something.

The process of changing a dog's behavior relies first and foremost on understanding and patience; successful positive training takes consistency, repetition, and following these general rules:

- Identify *why* your dog is doing what she is doing. You cannot effectively deal with a behavior unless you know the root cause.

- Once you know why, then you can ask yourself HOW to treat the behavior. To do this, it is vitally important that you understand your dog.

- Learn to communicate clearly. Effective two-way communication increases the bond between you.

- Find what motivates your dog and use this while teaching. Rewards in the form of food, toys, praise, or play are powerful, but every dog is different, so find out what motivates your dog the most.

- Be kind: never hit, scream at, or yank your dog. Do not combat fear with more fear—recognize your dog's concerns, then slowly and gently help her overcome them.

- Go very slowly when dealing with anxiety-related behaviors.

This may sound like common sense, but the concepts behind positive training are still relatively new in the context of our long relationship with dogs. Not even the most ardent supporter of punishment-based training can argue that it is more humane to punish than to reward, but some would argue that punishment in the form of an electric shock or a swift kick to a dog's ribs is no more damaging or inhumane than removing a favorite toy. There are degrees of punishment, and everyone must make their own choices about how far they're willing to go, but wouldn't you rather avoid doing anything that would make your dog feel pain or fear if you can help it, regardless of how minimal the resulting punishment might be?

How Dogs Learn

Traditional compulsion dog trainers sometimes argue that positive reinforcement doesn't work on more extreme behavior problems. Scientific study has now revealed what many of us had already deduced: when dealing with severe aggression and anxiety cases, reward-based, force-free positive reinforcement teaching is more effective and achieves longer-lasting results than punitive training methods.[1] When using positive reinforcement to deal with problem behaviors, several basic scientific principles are in play—most of which you will recognize from common life experiences, quite aside from dog interactions.

Although our dogs learn much the same way that we do, they live in our human world and their degree of success depends largely on the people who teach them. Dogs are good social learners, picking up cues and behaviors by watching and following the behavior of others. For example, Sadie has always loved to eat grass, chomping away at weeds and fescue with abandon on nearly every walk. Even though Jasmine had never experienced the apparent joys of this frustrating (for me) practice, she now eagerly follows her big brown best friend's lead and seeks out the tallest, sweetest vegetation on which to munch.

The way dogs learn also depends on genetics, instinct, hormones, senses, early experience with their mothers and littermates, and ending, ultimately, with us. Learning begins as soon as a puppy is born, and humans can help mold that early learning experience so that by the time a puppy is seven weeks old, she is ready to start exploring and learning about the world around her.

Effective learning can be compromised by poor health, solitary or overwhelming environments, forceful training methods, abuse, anxiety, fear, poor owner compliance, inconsistency, and lack of knowledge. Dogs are learning from their environment all the time—not just when you are teaching them.

CONDITIONING

.w of Effect confirms that behaviors resulting in ...nt outcomes will be repeated, whereas those that result in unpleasant consequences will decrease in frequency.[2] This is called *operant conditioning*. For example, when I ask Sadie to sit, she is rewarded with food or a toy. She is motivated to sit again in anticipation of a repeat reward. A word, hand signal, or both is then associated with the action of sitting.

Dogs also learn by association; this is known as *classical conditioning*. My dogs get excited each time I open a particular drawer because they've learned to associate the noise of the drawer opening with the appearance of their leashes, which almost always results in a walk. Now the leash is not only *associated* with the walk but also *reinforced* by the act of walking.

I use *counterconditioning* to teach unruly dogs more appropriate behavior. If a dog likes to run out the front door whenever it is opened, I counter the running behavior by teaching the dog to sit and stay some distance from the door whenever it is opened, which keeps the dog safe. Sadie used to have an unsavory habit of greeting guests by sticking her nose in people's crotches. I countered this by teaching her to get a toy whenever the doorbell rang so that she could only greet people with the toy in her mouth, which prevented her from sticking her snout in embarrassing places! Now whenever she hears the doorbell ring, she runs to get her toy first before heading for the front door to greet a guest.

Classical counterconditioning is a learning process used to help change a dog's emotional response toward a certain stimulus. For example, suppose my dog lunges aggressively at another dog she sees in the distance because she is fearful. Using classical counterconditioning, I pair the sight of the oncoming dog with something my dog likes (such as food or a toy), helping her associate the approaching dog with good things rather than fear of harm. Gradually she feels less fearful when she sees another dog. This works well as long as she is able to engage in behavior other than lunging. In this case, I would teach her an alternative cue, like sitting and looking at me as the dog approaches. The new cue then becomes an action she can focus on doing whenever she sees another dog. The sight of a dog, instead of causing fear, now triggers a different emotional and physical response, and instead of lunging, my dog immediately chooses to sit and look at me until the other dog passes by, whereupon she receives her reward. This kind of counterconditioning can help dogs adapt by gradually exposing them to a stimulus that previously triggered a reaction; when done sensitively, it allows learning to take place without a negative response.

CLICKER TRAINING

A clicker is a device that makes a unique clicking sound when pressed. When the sound is paired with something that the dog really loves, such as food or a toy, the dog makes the association between the sound and the reward; the clicking sound then becomes the precursor to a reward. The clicker is a valuable teaching device because there is no other sound like it in the dog's domestic world and, as it is processed quickly in the brain, it is an effective way to mark even the smallest of actions the dog makes. Small actions can then be shaped into a series of actions; the series can create a series of movements. For example, canine freestyle or "doggy dancing"—when dog and owner work together on an intricate series of moves (sometimes to music)—is a good example of what can be accomplished with clicker training. Clicker training is so versatile it can be used across the training spectrum, from teaching a puppy to sit to calming a reactive dog. The clicker is used not only to shape an action but also to mark positive changes in behavior and help dogs make better decisions in emotionally charged situations.

How to Encourage Your Dog to Listen to You

Understanding how your dog learns most effectively is the first step toward a healthy relationship and a well-mannered pet, but it's impossible to follow through on even the best intentions if you can't develop a consistent two-way line of communication with your dog. People often complain that their dogs don't listen to them, but when you think about it, how often is a dog really going to *want* to do what you're asking of her? Although you want her to come back to you from the other end of the park, she may be fully engaged in an investigation of a fascinating odor or in the midst of an important conversation with another dog.

Your goal should be to *matter* to your dog, and you can achieve this by being the source of good things in her life so that she gives you attention whenever you need it. People often emphasize a need for their dogs to be *obedient* rather than *cooperative*. Dog owners issue *commands* rather than focus on teaching the dog *cues* and attaching those cues to desired actions or behaviors. Motivating your dog to learn these cues by using rewards that make her feel good will go a long way toward producing the response you desire, even in the most distracting environments.

The Power of Food

People who discount the power of reward-based training frown on the use of food and claim that using rewards to teach dogs is tantamount to bribery. This frequently repeated claim completely disregards the scientific fact that food literally alters an animal's brain chemistry and also suggests a lack of understanding of basic scientific principles that support how reward-based training (conditioning) works.

Food has the power to help a dog learn and overcome any fear or anxiety she might have by raising the levels of dopamine in the brain, stimulating her desire to seek or move toward a reward. Dopamine is a neurotransmitter that plays a major role in reward-driven learning and helps regulate movement and emotional responses. When a dog is in the presence of a stimulus that scares her and is presented with food before she reaches a high level of stress, the food generates a positive emotional response. There are circuits in the dog's brain that encourage seeking or hunting behavior and circuits that elicit the fear response. When you present food to your dog, you turn on her seeker system, effectively turning off the fear.[3] This is one reason why when teaching activities such as scent work, using food is so valuable for fearful dogs. Turning on the thinking brain deactivates the emotional brain, enhancing a dog's attentiveness with positive motivation and allowing her to move into a calmer state in which learning can take place. In other words, because food is incompatible with fear, using food for teaching is incredibly effective, especially when it comes to modifying a dog's anxiety and stress.

The food you use to motivate your dog to learn must be of high value until she is responding reliably. Once this has been achieved, you can start using the high-value food intermittently, which means that your dog doesn't always get it when she responds to a cue but receives an alternate, lower-value reward instead. Because your dog is unsure of when she'll get the high-value food again, she continues to respond in anticipation of getting it the next time she does what is asked of her.

Such intermittent reinforcement actually makes your dog respond more quickly and reliably because this learning is based on the same concept that makes a casino slot machine so addictive. It would be wonderful if a slot machine gave out money every time you played it, but unfortunately that doesn't happen. The potential, however, that you could win the jackpot with the very next pull of the lever makes you want to play even more.

Multi-Motivators

Even though food treats are a really effective training tool, some dogs are motivated by other rewards, such as toys, play, praise, or simply being touched. I have trained many dogs using different types of rewards—a game of tug, a kind word, or a "life reward," such as a walk. I also like to vary rewards so the dog never knows what is coming next or use what I call *multimotivators*, such as a food/toy/praise combination. Whatever you decide to use, a reward is going to make learning fun for your dog, improve her confidence, and build up a strong bond between you.

Remember that the key to cooperation and compliance is trust and motivation, so the more exciting and valuable you appear to be to your dog, the more she will listen to you in every situation. When you are in a new, unfamiliar environment, however, don't be surprised if your dog ignores you because she's not comfortable—all her mental and physical energy is most likely being spent on ensuring she is safe. Be aware of how the environment affects her ability to pay attention to you and know that if she is having difficulty, it may not be because she is simply choosing to ignore you.

Is Your Dog Hard to Teach?

Clients often tell me that their dog is stubborn, hard to train, or lacks intelligence—but in most cases the owner simply hasn't found a way to encourage the learning process or harness the dog's potential. Finding the right motivator is key, and although physical enrichment is vital in the learning process, mental stimulation is equally important.

When a dog is learning, blood flow to the brain increases, bringing energy to nerve cells. But using up this mental energy can be tiring, so keep sessions short to help your dog maintain focus, and keep in mind that each dog learns at her own pace—it is up to you to find out what that pace is. Dogs also love predictability, so always be consistent to avoid confusion. For example, if you don't allow your dog up on the sofa, make sure that all members of your household follow that rule. Be patient and flexible with your expectations, and be prepared for failure—it is an important part of the learning process. Finally, once your dog has learned a particular action or behavior, continue to reinforce it in everyday life, and never miss a chance to reward behavior that you like, even if it's just a simple "good girl"—your dog will love you for it!

3

LEADING WITHOUT FORCE
The Future of Dog Training

A great leader is one who can positively affect the behavior of others without using force, like Mahatma Gandhi and Martin Luther King, Jr. These men were able to alter the course of history and humankind's progress without firing a gun or raising a fist. Many people suggest that positive dog trainers lack strength of will or the power to effect change, but the ability to redirect the misbehavior of the biggest, strongest, most aggressive dogs, without the use of force, is actually much more powerful than using punitive methods.

Our goal is to teach, guide, and influence our dogs so they choose to behave in a positive way. We don't want to get caught up in this desperate need to show we are the "alpha" or "boss." We just want our dogs to be happy, fulfilled, and well-mannered.

Yet some people still think that if a dog walks in front of them or tries to get through the door first, it must be a sign that he wants to be in charge. In fact, dogs naturally walk faster than us because they have four legs and we have only two and they're just excited to get where they're headed! If the way they walk bothers us, it's our job to help them learn to control their pace and excitement levels. If we don't want dogs to pull on the leash because it's uncomfortable, unsafe, or just really annoying, we must help them learn to change. We celebrate the purity of emotion in our pets, yet sometimes we mistakenly assign human insecurities to the simple joys they relish so innocently.

By now you can see how words like "alpha" and "dominance" have caused a great deal of confusion in the dog training profession and untold amounts of stress for our dogs. If you want to have a good relationship with your dog, show true leadership by rewarding good behavior, instilling self-confidence, and influencing behavior without the use of force. Positive reinforcement behavioral principles can work with any breed of dog and with any issue, from teaching a puppy to learn how to sit to rehabilitating an aggressive or "red zone" dog.

I remain concerned about the example some old-school trainers are setting for the new generation of dog owners, trainers, and handlers. And, as a mother and a regular speaker in schools, I am also aware of how children are influenced by a respected adult. According to noted clinical psychologist Dr. Paula Bloom, treating animals harshly in front of children can be very damaging and sets a terrible precedent.[1]

I saw this firsthand at a big dog event attended by a large group of eager, dog-loving kids. Toward the end of the day, a K9 police dog handler passed by with her gorgeous German Shepherd, and naturally we all stopped to admire him—just as he decided to sniff the ground by his side. As he put his head down, the handler gave a quick, forceful yank on the leash. The scent the dog had found, however, proved to be too tempting, and again his head went down to sniff it. This time the officer lifted the leash and jerked the dog so hard that all four paws came off the ground and he yelped in pain. The kids gasped in shock, and the officer angrily cursed him. Never one to be mistaken for a quiet bystander, I knew I had to do something. I approached and asked why she had yanked her dog so hard, but she didn't take kindly to my question, demanding that I move out of her way. Instead, I stood my ground and calmly asked her what kind of example she thought she was setting to the children who had just witnessed her abusing her dog. She was unable to offer any kind of explanation for her behavior and pushed passed me, shamefaced and angry. The children were appalled and visibly shaken by witnessing such mistreatment.

As parents, teachers, and adults, we need to work out how we can best handle ourselves and appropriately manage the influence we have on others. Some may value a dog's obedience more than the relationship, but I'm glad I'm not one of them. I want a well-behaved dog as much as the next person, but I'll find other ways to ensure that happens without the use of force.

Fear of Change

I am blessed to have a large, multifaceted public platform and, as you can see, I'm very vocal about the need to move toward humane training methods. But the more I speak about the need for change, the more I open myself up to criticism from those who still practice punitive methods. The more harshly these critics react, the more their vitriol exposes an underlying desperation to justify, defend, and hang on to the old ways that seem to be slipping away. As with ongoing battles to overcome injustices such as racism and sexism, it is very hard for generations of people to change their deep-seated beliefs and to admit that there might be another, better way of doing things. I'm not suggesting that our societal struggle over the evils of racism is on a par with a debate over how to train dogs, but the principles in play are much the same. It takes time for a culture to change, but those who are willing to investigate other avenues are most often the ones responsible for moving society forward. For every naysayer who attempts to discredit the progress we've made in our understanding of dog behavior, there are many who celebrate how humane training has changed the lives of their dogs for the better. Although counteracting entrenched views is difficult, the beauty and effectiveness of reward-based training provides a daily reminder that we can make a dog's learning and life experience better by moving toward a kinder way of teaching.

A large part of my job as a dog trainer is to find out what motivates both dog and owner. Almost daily, I deal with intimate human situations in the families that I work with. These situations can include infertility, alcoholism, social dysfunction, apathy, and abuse. As any good dog trainer will tell you, we must be able to identify and manage not only dog problems but also human issues, and though we're not formally trained to do so, our to-do list with new clients often includes some level of psychological assessment.

Even so, I continue to be baffled by one particular human weakness that unfortunately I see all too often: an unwillingness to change, despite evidence and overwhelming natural instinct. As Dr. Paula Bloom explains, "People are susceptible to the influence of people they respect—i.e., a professional—and the trust that they put into this person to impart the right knowledge causes them to remain silent even if they are uncomfortable with the way their family member is being handled. People who dominate may have a family history of being dominated themselves, and because it is naturally difficult for us to feel powerless, we attempt to counteract this with control. People like to be in charge and will defend even a flawed theory if it aligns internally with something that makes them feel right. Despite contradictory evidence, many people are not particularly interested in educating themselves about ideas that might dissuade them from their deeply held belief."[2]

Owners often seem to feel that having a poorly behaved dog reflects badly on themselves. When I go into clients' homes, they regularly apologize to me about their dogs' behavior. Their dogs embarrass them, and this embarrassment provokes anger, which is then directed at the dog in the form of punishment.

Some people may simply enjoy the feeling of power and control that dominating gives them. We have all encountered such bullies in our lives. A bully's fear and insecurity manifests itself in a need to control others. Even though bullies seem strong and in charge, their behavior betrays an underlying weakness and inability to cope.

How many times since becoming a dog trainer have I witnessed other trainers and owners using physical or emotional manipulation to exert control over the dogs they are handling because, like bullies, they are insecure or fear losing control? It's harder to combat because our culture celebrates outward shows of strength, and winning the battle is everything, even if the animal being dominated is under severe stress. I regularly weather critiques of positive training that reveal an impatience and unwillingness to treat dogs with the respect they deserve. For example, during one relatively quick and simple demonstration of getting a young puppy to learn how to sit using positive techniques, a small minority were apparently maddened that I didn't forcibly push the pup's rear onto the ground while saying the word "sit." Instead of relishing the opportunity to encourage a young dog to problem solve for himself and experience the joy of learning how to "get it right," they wanted me to take control. Dominant control appeals to people's desire for quick results and instant gratification. Force, fear, and pain are quick motivators for dogs, and many take advantage of that.

Not all trainers and owners who teach dogs in this way are insecure and desire absolute control. Many are lovely people who genuinely think that using forceful training methods is the only way to train dogs. They probably don't realize that what they are doing is damaging in any way. The mother who pushes her child in a stroller while walking her dog on a prong collar, the elderly woman who has her dog on a shock collar to prevent him from chasing squirrels, the millions of people who contain their dogs with electric fences—all use quick fixes designed simply to make their lives with dogs as easy as possible, but the damage these methods are causing is immense.

The Future of Dog Training

As a scientist friend of mine is fond of saying, the great thing about scientific fact is that you are free to disagree with it, but you'll be wrong.

Though the argument rages on, the debate is over. The world's top scientists and behaviorists as well as the most respected veterinary institutions are now warning the public against using compulsion training and are encouraging owners and trainers to use positive reinforcement methods instead. In a position statement, the American Veterinary Society of Animal Behavior (AVSAB) has declared "that veterinarians not refer clients to trainers or behavior consultants who coach and advocate dominance hierarchy theory and the subsequent confrontational training that follows from it."[3] The AVSAB further states that animal behavior training should follow the scientifically based guidelines of positive reinforcement, operant conditioning, classical conditioning, desensitization, and counterconditioning.

But old habits are hard to change. It generally takes twenty years for new ideas to be fully accepted by the general public. Assuming that timeline is correct, I certainly hope that within a decade all dog trainers and owners will have switched to using positive methods—I know our dogs will thank us for it. As Mech states, this isn't just an issue of semantics and political correctness. Rather, "it is one of biological correctness that accurately captures the biological and social role of the animals rather than perpetuate a faulty view."[4]

It boils down to this—what kind of relationship do you want to build with your dog? A true bond is built on trust, which can easily be destroyed when dominance techniques are used. Dogs are thinking, emotional beings with the ability to solve problems and make the right choices if we offer them the appropriate guidance. You have the power to enhance these abilities with humane teaching techniques and give your dog the chance to be successful in a domestic world. Throw outdated dominance theory out of the window and embrace modern methods of teaching. You and your dog will be glad you did.

BUILDING THE BOND

Understanding Canine Language

You cannot build a strong bond with your dog unless you truly understand how she perceives the world around her, but to do this effectively you must first learn her language. This chapter will take you deep into your dog's mind, giving you the foundation you need to build a stronger relationship and making it easier for you to find effective positive solutions for any problem behaviors your dog might have.

I was particularly drawn to a career working with dogs in part to understand how and why we humans came to have such a strong and sustaining bond with *Canis familiaris*. For thousands of years dogs have hunted with us, protected our lands, warned us of impending danger, and brought us comfort. The shared need we both developed for nurture and companionship meant that dogs became more attuned to humans than to any other species.

Dogs and humans are biologically similar, because both species are ultimately driven by their emotional responses. When we pet a dog lovingly, for example, the warmth and happiness we feel comes from a release into the bloodstream of oxytocin—

a "bonding" hormone that has a powerful effect on dogs and humans. Dr. Kerstin Uvnas-Moberg, a doctor and professor of physiology and a pioneer in the study of oxytocin, studied this hormone release by taking blood samples from dogs and their owners before and during a petting session.[1] When owners stroked their dogs, they had a release of oxytocin similar to what mothers experience while nursing babies. Interestingly, petting also triggered a burst of oxytocin in the dogs themselves. Miho Nagasawah, of the Department of Animal Science and Biotechnology at Azabu University in Japan, showed that even eye contact between a dog and a human causes an increase in oxytocin.[2] This interaction between our two species has a powerful physiological effect on both of us, promoting feelings of love and attachment while lowering blood pressure and heart rate, soothing pain, and lessening stress. Studies have shown that people who have dogs are less likely to suffer from a heart attack and are three to four times more likely to survive one if they do.[3]

Dogs are so bonded with us that they, like humans, show a relatively high level of social intelligence. Dogs can mimic our behavior and read our facial expressions the same way we attempt to read theirs, enabling us to connect on an emotional level despite our tendency to find each other's language confusing. When humans look at a person's face, their eyes tend to wander to the left, falling on the right-hand side of the face. This "left gaze bias" happens only when we encounter faces, not objects, because the right side of the human face is better at expressing our emotional state. Studies at the University of Lincoln in the United Kingdom have shown that dogs also have this left gaze bias, but for them it happens only when looking at a human face—not an object or the face of another dog. Researchers believe that dogs developed this skill through their relationship with humans, possibly as a way to protect themselves from human anger or threat.[4]

In addition to our ability to form social relationships, another bonding trait shared by both humans and dogs is our love of play. Play develops social skills, is important for mental and physical growth, allows us to enjoy activities that make us feel good, and enhances the connection between us.

Canine Intelligence

Buster, a food-obsessed Terrier, was one of the smartest dogs I've ever met. His owners had constructed a barricade in their home designed to prevent Buster from getting into the kitchen and stealing food from the countertops, but somehow he always found ingenious ways to break through it. His problem-solving skills were so advanced that even when faced with seemingly impossible new challenges, he ultimately found new ways to solve them. For example, thanks to his nifty nose and his odd desire to urinate on the kitchen appliances, Buster had perfected a rather novel approach to getting onto the countertop, which we discovered by setting up remote cameras in the kitchen area and watching what they captured live from another room. This clever little dog was too small to simply jump up onto the counter; instead he used his paws to scrabble open the oven door and jump onto it. From this vantage point he opened a drawer next to the oven, and from there it was an easy leap onto the kitchen countertop. Buster proceeded to open anything that might contain food (including the microwave and cookie jar), ate whatever he could find, then promptly and contentedly relieved himself on the bread container. Nothing was safe if Buster was left alone in the kitchen.

As I have previously stated, a dog's ability to solve problems and make choices is comparable to that of a two-year-old human child—far beyond the capabilities of most other animals. But although comparing canine and human intelligence may provide us with valuable insight, it does not take into account dogs' exceptional sensory capabilities and problem-solving skills. Dogs like Buster are very good at adapting to different situations, identifying problems in their environment, and coming up with further clever solutions if needed.

In addition to being great problem solvers, dogs have exceptional physical skills, moving their bodies fluidly through daily life while still understanding the parameters of what they can and cannot do. They also have an amazing ability to understand and respond to cue words that we give them—provided we teach them correctly.

Dogs have very good memories. Oxytocin is the hormone responsible for social memory, enabling dogs to recognize people and other animals they have previously met, thereby allowing them to retain social attachments. Dogs also remember, among other things, where they have hidden a bone; where their leash is hung; associations among words, objects, and actions; and emotionally significant life events. Here's an example. While hiking through the North Georgia mountains one summer day, Sadie was stung by a bee. The experience was so traumatic for her that now, whenever she hears or sees a bee, her tail goes between her legs and she runs away. Six months later, in the dead of winter, we were walking along the same mountain path, and as soon as we approached the creek bend where she had been stung, Sadie's ears went back and she took off. I looked around to see what had scared her and then realized we were at the very place where she had been stung the previous summer. Not only had she made an association between the sound of a bee and feeling pain, but she also remembered the exact place where the traumatic event had happened.

Body Language

Dogs communicate with us and each other by using a complex system of body signals that we humans often miss or don't understand. Before I start working with any client, I spend time simply observing their dogs with them, because it always surprises me how little people know about how their dogs communicate. Gradually, my clients gain a new appreciation for the canine experience by watching how their dogs "talk," and the changes they make in response to what they see often improve the human/canine relationship dramatically.

Misreading a dog's signals can lead to confusion and conflict. One dramatic example of misreading and misunderstanding behavior was the case of a Chihuahua, Niles, who lived with Karen, a lovely lady in Birmingham, England. Previously Karen had only ever owned cats, but when her last beloved cat died, she decided it was time to get a dog. She picked a Chihuahua mainly because, as she sheepishly admitted, the breed is roughly the same size as a cat. After a relatively normal start in life, Niles developed a chronic aversion to being touched, eventually hating to be handled so much that he bit Karen each time she attempted to get close to him.

Karen loved Niles but couldn't understand why her beloved dog didn't feel the same. He followed her everywhere, slept on her bed, and became anxious when she left, but he simply would not let Karen near him when she wanted to show him affection. I watched Niles with fascination as he snarled and bared his teeth at us, because he was one of the best canine communicators I'd ever seen. Niles wore his heart on his paw and clearly signaled his intentions, so I was amazed that Karen misunderstood what he was trying to say. From the beginning of my time with them, I knew this relationship was salvageable as long as Karen developed a clearer understanding of canine body language.

Whenever Karen approached, Niles turned his head sideways but kept his eyes firmly fixed on her. His mouth closed tightly as he took a step back, turned his body away, and lifted his front paw. If Karen continued to approach, he blinked rapidly, licked his lips, tucked his tail between his legs, and froze. When she reached out to touch him, his lip curled so that his teeth were exposed; he growled deeply and then snapped. As soon as Karen moved away from him, Niles stood up tall, raised his tail, and shook his body as if trying to get water off his back.

I found out that because Karen had loved stroking her cats, poor Niles had been petted continually as a puppy. Though tolerant of this at first, he had grown tired of the constant handling. When his peaceful "back off" signals didn't work, Niles learned that snapping and biting was the only effective way to get Karen to back away from him. He lived in fear of being handled, making it very hard for her to even attach the leash onto his collar and take him for a walk.

The situation did indeed seem desperate, but within the space of a few hours, the relationship between Karen and Niles took a dramatic turn. It was a great relief for her to learn that the remedy was a relatively simple one and that she no longer had to battle with what she thought was a dominant dog.

To understand how I solved this conundrum, let's delve in to some relevant background information. Dogs communicate using a complex language of body signals that reflect what they are thinking and feeling. These signals are used, consciously and unconsciously, to communicate intent and ensure personal safety by *positively* affecting behavior in others. One dog might try to appease another by actively seeking attention via one or more of the following behaviors: muzzle and/or ear licking, jumping up, lowering and curving the body, blinking, clacking or exposing the teeth ("smiling"), lip licking, lowering the head and ears, or

play bowing. Although much appeasement consists of ac
language, passive submission such as cowering and boo
ing seems to be a response to escalating fear in the presen
perceived threat. A socially experienced dog receiving these signals will tolerate this language of appeasement and reciprocate
with appropriate signals; other, less experienced dogs might take
advantage of this deference and attempt to control or aggress.

In addition to appeasement, dogs commonly use displacement
signals to avoid confrontation. These signals are used during an
uncomfortable or stressful situation to provide a distraction and to
cover up what the dog is really feeling. Yawning, sniffing, scratching, sneezing, and licking are all active behaviors that also keep
dogs calm. I use similar displacement behaviors when I first go into
the homes of dogs that are fearful and/or aggressive toward
humans. Rather than having any visual or physical contact with the
dog, I pretend to read a magazine, write on a clipboard, or look at a
book. These activities take my attention away from the dog, which
relieves pressure by providing something else for her to focus on.
These displacement activities also help mask any tension I may be
feeling and keep my body language fluid and my breathing relaxed.
Dogs easily pick up on human tension, so even standing with my
weight on one hip and breathing normally while "reading" a book
helps a dog relax in my presence. I sometimes have owners teach
their guests this behavior when entering the home of a dog that is
fearful of strangers, and I find it works wonders.

Some dogs show ultimate deference by urinating or by rolling over and exposing their bellies. Misinterpreting a common
signal like this can lead to disastrous results. During filming for
the pilot episode of *It's Me or the Dog*, Blue, a nervous Old English
Sheepdog, rolled over and showed his stomach to a construction
worker working on the house next door. Mistakenly assuming
that Blue wanted his belly rubbed, the man crouched down and

began stroking him, only to be swiftly bitten on the hand. Far from inviting the stranger to pet him by freely exposing the most vulnerable part of his body, Blue was actually offering an appeasement gesture in the hope that the man would go away. From his point of view, once the man seemingly ignored these signals, Blue felt he had no choice but to bite in order to protect himself. Some socially inexperienced dogs may not always recognize the signals that other dogs give them, but humans certainly have much to learn and fewer excuses for getting it wrong.

Tail wagging is another frequently misinterpreted signal. Most people believe that a wagging tail means that a dog is happy, which of course is true in many cases, but some dogs also wag their tails when aroused, overstimulated, and frustrated. You can usually tell the difference by looking at what the rest of the body is doing:

- A confident or aroused dog will hold her tail in the air, allowing scent from the anal glands to circulate more freely and advertise her presence.
- A dog that is wagging her tail but barking with a defensive body posture, tense face, and hard staring eyes is overly aroused and frustrated, which means that she should not be approached.
- A tail that is held low or between the legs signals a lack of confidence, nervousness, or fear.
- A tail that is held high but wagged more slowly means that the dog is curious and assessing a situation.
- A tail that is extended and curved means that the dog is tense and ready to take offensive or defensive action.
- A tail that wags around and around like a helicopter and is accompanied by relaxed fluid body movement and a wiggling bottom signals friendliness and a willingness to engage.

- Research has shown that when a dog sees a person she likes, her tail wags more to the right. When she sees an unfamiliar person, her tail wags more to the left. Subtle body language like this is easy to miss.

The tail is important for both balance and signaling, which is why the practice of tail docking, or partial removal of a dog's tail, is so harmful. Because the tail is a prime indicator of mood, dogs with docked tails are unable to communicate properly with that part of their body, meaning that other dogs and people miss vital signals.

Niles used many of the signals I have described to appease and distract his owner, but until I made Karen aware, it seemed as though they were usually just ignored. Karen was so intent on showing Niles that she was the boss in the relationship that she was oblivious to his tension. She paid the price by receiving some nasty bites.

I wanted Karen to show Niles that she understood and respected his wishes by giving him much-needed space. I knew paying him less attention and giving him some room would relieve the pressure he felt, and in time he would be comfortable enough to seek out attention from her. At first Niles was a little confused with the change in Karen's behavior, but after a few days he began to approach her. When a nervous and fearful dog realizes he has some control over a situation, he gains confidence. Karen was to praise him whenever she saw him relax, and if he asked for attention, she acknowledged it with vocal communication only. Even when Niles came to sit beside her or on her lap, he felt comfortable because he knew he could do so without being touched. Gradually, as trust slowly developed between them, Karen gently handled him, rewarding his calm acceptance with gentle praise and a food treat. Starting with one touch at a time and building up gradually helped Niles appreciate close contact.

Karen now understood his language so well that she responded appropriately whenever she sensed that Niles had had enough.

The issue of attaching the leash was also easily resolved. Instead of fumbling with his collar, I gave Karen a clothbound slip leash that she was able to casually slip over his neck as she walked past him, under the pretence of doing something else. Because Niles never knew when the leash was coming, he never showed any signs of stress. As soon as the leash was around his neck he happily went outside. I don't like to use slip leashes as a general rule because of their tendency to tighten around a dog's neck, so as soon as we were outside, I showed Karen how to attach his regular leash and remove the slip. Because Niles was so distracted in a more stimulating environment, he never showed any negative reaction to this change. Karen continued with this strategy for a month until she got to the point where she could attach the leash to his collar inside the house with no problem. She also taught Niles action cues such as "sit," "lie down," and "touch," rewarding him for his compliance. Niles loved and responded well to these training sessions.

Touch training or "targeting" is useful in many situations and helps nervous dogs accept a person's touch or see an approaching hand as something positive rather than a threat. It's also a great cue to motivate a dog to come when called. This cue should be taught to every puppy and dog to prevent hand shyness from ever developing.

Teaching the Touch Cue

- Dogs are naturally curious animals, so start this technique by presenting your hand to your dog. As she goes to investigate your hand and touches it with her nose, praise and reward her.

- Take your hand away, put it behind your back, w; or two, and then present it again.
- Repeat this exercise until your dog is touching your hand whenever you present it.
- When your dog is good at this task, start adding the word "touch" as she goes to touch your hand with her nose. After many repetitions you will find that she will respond as soon as you ask her to "touch."
- Try this exercise with both hands so that she gets used to touching either one.
- When she is reliably touching your hand, use this cue around the home. Call your dog to come to you, and as she gets close, extend your hand and ask her to "touch."
- Every touch should be rewarded at this point—some with praise and others with a treat.
- When your dog is responding well indoors, take the exercise outside where there are more distractions.
- Gradually increase the distance between you so that your dog has to travel farther to touch your hand.

Niles's behavior changed rapidly, and Karen was amazed. Within a month, a dysfunctional relationship had turned into one that was mutually respectful, because both dog and owner finally understood each other and became more confident in the other's presence. Niles's newfound security meant he no longer reacted defensively to being touched and actively encouraged a more hands-on relationship.

Common Canine Body Language

Any signal a dog demonstrates must always be read in the context of whatever other body signals or vocal language the dog is displaying at the time. Similar signals have different meanings in different situations, so the position of the body and other vocal signals will help you work out a dog's intent and emotional state.

STRESS/DISCOMFORT/NERVOUS LANGUAGE

- Yawning—a commonly misunderstood stress signal
- Lip licking or tongue flicking—a quick flick of the tongue or lick of the lips can signal stress
- Micro body freezing—the dog freezes for a few seconds before reacting
- Body freezing—the dog freezes until the threat goes away or she decides to use fight or flight
- Whale eye—the dog turns her head away but keeps looking at the perceived threat, showing the whites of her eyes
- Head turn—the dog turns her head away from a fear source
- Furrowed brow and curved eyebrows—caused by facial tension
- Tense jaw—the mouth is closed as the dog prepares for action
- Hugging—a dog may gain comfort by holding onto her owner
- Low tail carriage—indicates discomfort and uncertainty
- Curved tongue—the tongue is curved at the edges from tension
- Raspy, dry-sounding panting—nervousness can reduce saliva production

- Twitching whiskers—caused by facial tension
- Shaking—caused by adrenaline release
- Drooling—stress can also cause excessive salivation
- Lack of focus—an anxious dog finds learning difficult
- Sweaty paws—dogs sweat through their foot pads
- Piloerection—the hair on a dog's neck and spine stands on end (like human goose bumps), making the dog appear bigger while releasing odor from the glands contained in the hair follicles

APPEASEMENT/DEFERENCE LANGUAGE— DESIGNED TO APPEASE OTHERS

- Head bobbing or lowering
- Head turning
- Averting eyes
- Lip licking
- Low tail carriage
- Tail tucked between the legs
- Curved and lowered body
- Stomach flip—the dog flips quickly onto her back, exposing her stomach, signaling that she is withdrawing from interaction

CURIOUS/ANTICIPATORY LANGUAGE

- Head cocked to one side or the other
- Front paw lifted—the dog is anticipating what might happen and what action she should take
- Mouth closed—the dog is sizing up the situation in preparation for action

DISPLACEMENT LANGUAGE (WHICH HELPS TO SELF-CALM AND REFOCUS ATTENTION AWAY FROM THE DOG AND ONTO SOMETHING ELSE)

- Sneezing
- Shaking
- Sniffing
- Nose licking
- Yawning
- Spinning
- Pacing
- Chattering teeth
- Shake off—release of stress and tension

DEFENSIVE AND OFFENSIVE LANGUAGE

- Body leaning forward
- Tense mouth
- Lips vibrating as the dog growls
- Air snapping—the dog snaps in the air to warn something to back away
- Snapping with skin contact—also a warning to back away
- Fast nip—an immediate bite and release with bruising or slight wound, telling a threat to back off
- Deeper bite—a dog that bites with more intensity is intending to harm
- Bite and hold—intent to harm
- Bite, hold, and shake—intent to harm and potentially kill (Some dogs will bite, hold, shake, and disembowel stuffed toys, simulating the killing of prey; while this is prevalent among dogs with high prey drive, even dogs with low drive

can indulge in behavior of this type. If your dog likes to disembowel stuffed toys, this doesn't mean she wants to do the same to a person or animal. Sadie loves to disembowel toys, but she is very gentle with people, especially children.)

- Hard, staring eyes

RELAXED LANGUAGE

- Mouth slightly open, tongue relaxed and lolling to one side
- Small body freezes during play
- Play bow—this signal invites play and tells others that whatever action comes next is still just play
- Turning over, inviting belly rub—showing trust and enjoying social contact
- Relaxed facial expression
- Squinty or blinking eyes
- Tail wagging fast, either side to side or in a round motion like a helicopter
- Wiggling backside

The Value of Dog-to-Dog and Human-Dog Play

Sadie and Jasmine love to play together. Their size difference doesn't seem to affect their ability to enjoy one another; they just make it work. Sadie lies down on her side with her mouth open as Jasmine jumps around her head putting her tiny Chihuahua mouth on parts of Sadie's large muzzle. Both dogs make a lot of noise during their mock battle, showing their teeth and flashing the whites of their eyes. Then as quickly as it starts, play stops—for a brief moment. Sadie sneezes, and Jasmine turns around to lick her flank before leaping back to spar with her best friend.

Dog-to-dog play is a series of active and repetitive behaviors that have different meanings depending on context. These behaviors help dogs develop important life skills and experiences that promote good physical and mental health. Because safe play relies on the dog's ability to read vocal and body signals, dogs that don't have the opportunity to play are usually deficient when it comes to communicating and identifying these signals. These dogs tend to play rudely: body slamming, mouthing too hard, mounting, and generally causing mayhem. Most well-socialized dogs are quite adept at playing and reading social language in others, and while some will tolerate rude play behavior, others will only take so much battering from a rambunctious bully. If your dog is pushy or plays too rough, interaction with other dogs should cease until she learns to greet and play nicely. Teaching a reliable recall will help keep play appropriate because calling your dog back before things get too rowdy will give her time to calm down before reintroducing her back into the group.

Appropriate play can be rough, but human intervention is usually not needed. As long as each dog allows the other to win and lose the game, the potential for conflict is avoided. The more aroused dogs become, however, the more likely it is that the mock battle will turn into something more serious. Good players are confident and actively seek out other dogs to play with, maintaining order during play by using clear signals so that the dogs they're playing with don't become too aroused or overwhelmed.

Play begins in puppyhood and helps puppies develop good coordination while allowing them to practice a series of exaggerated behaviors that promote social ease. The beauty of play is that for most dogs the desire to interact with others in such a manner continues into adulthood. Sadie is now ten years old, yet when she

dives into her play bow and runs around with her mouth w
her tongue hanging to one side, and a twinkle in her eye,
as vibrant as a young pup. Both my dogs have learned to p_y ___ly
with each other, relying on a series of cut-off signals that communicate their peaceful intentions. Play bows, sniffing, sneezing, yawning, itching, and licking occur for brief moments throughout play
to communicate that any future action is still just play.

Playing with dogs also helps increase the human-animal
bond. Most dogs love to play a game of fetch or tug of war with
their owners and like to use their supreme sense of smell to locate
hidden objects. There are many fantastic activities you can do
with your dog that cater to her instinctive drive to seek out food
or prey. Because Sadie is a Labrador, she loves to retrieve things
that I hide for her and is particularly fond of locating toys that I
dab with duck scent. Fortunately for Sadie this scent comes in a
bottle I can buy at my local pet shop. The scent motivates her to
search for any toy that I put it on. I call this activity the "go find it"
game. Here is how you play it:

- Begin by dabbing a little scent on a toy and hiding it.
- Allow your dog to see where you hide the toy.
- Dab some of the same scent on a piece of cloth and let your
  dog smell it.
- Tell your dog to "go find" the toy.
- If your dog has trouble locating the "hide," guide her with
  encouragement to the place where the toy is "hidden" and
  praise her when she finds it.
- Make hides easy to begin with by placing the toy closer;
  then, as she becomes more proficient, gradually increase the
  distance between your dog and the hide.

- When she is finding the hide reliably, take her away from the area and hide the toy so that she can't see where you are hiding it.
- Encourage her to "go find" again.
- If your dog likes to scent the ground, you can make it easier for her to find the toy by dabbing some scent on the ground leading to the area where it is hidden.

There are many great games for dogs that like to chase things, my favorite being "toy on a stick." This toy can be purchased or made at home by attaching a soft toy to some rope, tying it to a stick, and whirling it around your body. Both my dogs love this game, and ten minutes of chasing tires them out for hours. Jasmine also loves to chase birds and squirrels, and "toy on a stick" actually helps me cue when she can chase them. Before the game starts, I point my finger in her direction and tell her to "wait." Jasmine has to be completely still for a short period of time until I give her the cue to "go chase" the toy. This game translates well when I have her outside in an off-leash area. If it's safe for her to indulge in her favorite pastime—chasing squirrels—then I allow her to do so, but only on my cue. If the time is not appropriate, I use the wait signal and attach her leash to redirect her to something else. She has now learned to respond to "wait" even if the cue doesn't always end in an opportunity to chase, because the potential to indulge in the passion is often reinforced. I'm a great believer in allowing dogs to satisfy their instinctive needs if appropriate, but having the behavior occur on cue means I can safely control Jasmine in any environment.

I believe one of the reasons why we connect with dogs so well is our mutual desire to play. Any activity, whether it's a simple ᵇur backyard or something you do with your dog as a ., will keep you both mentally and physically fit while building a stronger relationship between you. Allowing your dog to play with other dogs in your household and organizing play dates with canine friends will help your dog rehearse valuable play behavior and maintain healthy social skills.

Canine Senses

To truly understand how dogs perceive the world, it is important to learn about their sensory experience. Senses are closely linked to emotions, and emotions drive behavior, so it stands to reason that even though we are just scratching the surface when it comes to understanding the dog's sense capabilities, they play an integral part in the dog's experience. I love using the senses to help dogs learn and work through any behavioral issues they might have—a process I call *sensory education*.

SIGHT

A dog's visual system does not dominate the brain as it does in humans, meaning that dogs are less reliant on sight for information. However, breeds such as Retrievers, Sighthounds, and Sheepdogs are very good at detecting even the smallest movements in the distance, and they rely on this ability to detect moving prey and retrieve game. Because dogs are much lower to the ground than humans, they obviously see the world from a very different perspective. People who own small dogs tend to forget what the world must look like to them, so lying on the ground helps shed a little light on their small dog's visual experience.

Humans can see about 180 degrees around them, whereas dogs, depending on their eye placement, can see approximately 250 degrees, especially if their eyes are located more toward the side of their heads. Dogs are able to see much better in dim light because the central portion of the dog's retina is composed primarily of rod cells that see in shades of gray, whereas human central retinas primarily have cone cells that perceive color. Rods need much less light to function than cones do. The tapetum, a mirror-like structure in the back of a dog's eye that reflects light, gives the retina a second chance to register light that has entered the eye. It is thought that a dog can see four times better than a human in low light, which provides an ideal environment for catching prey. Dogs also have what is known as *dichromatic vision,* meaning they see only part of the range of colors in the visual spectrum of light wavelength. They are unable to see the red to green spectrum but can see in shades of yellow and blue. I've never understood why so many dog toys are colored red when both red and green appear as gray or black to a dog. So a red toy on green grass just looks like gray on more gray, which explains why some dogs don't see toys that are thrown for them even though the difference in color looks very obvious to us.

Dogs have a third eyelid that acts like a windshield wiper, clearing debris from the eye—much needed when you are closer to the ground. Large pupils mean that dogs don't have great depth of field in their vision, so when looking at things in the distance, they can focus clearly only on objects in the center of their vision. Everything else around this center is blurry. In dim light, the dog's vision degrades from 20/20 to 25/70. This means dogs can see fine details only to a maximum distance of twenty feet away, whereas a person with good eyesight can see them at seventy-five feet. This limitation probably explains why Jasmine has a hard time recognizing a family member coming toward her until they wave their arms or come closer. Active hand signals are easy to see and recognize even from far away.

HEARING

Have you ever seen your dog suddenly cock her head to one side as if she is listening to something? How about when she shoots up and barks at the wall or runs to the front door to welcome a family member home well before the car turns into the driveway and the door is opened? The human ear can detect frequencies of up to 20,000 Hertz (Hz), whereas dogs can hear frequencies up to 45,000 to 67,000 Hz.[5] This makes them more effective hunters, locating hidden prey just from the high-pitched squeaks small animals make. Jasmine often tilts her head to one side and then pounces on the ground in front of her, digging furiously to get to whatever she has heard burrowing; her Terrier ears pick up the slightest sound of prey deep underneath her. Dogs with pricked ears can better detect a sound source than drop-eared breeds, but all dogs can move their ears around like satellite dishes, picking up sound from every direction.

Puppies are born deaf, but their ears open at two weeks of age, and by one month their hearing is exceptional. However, noted sound researcher Joshua Leeds believes that because sound is absorbed through the entire body, a puppy may actually be able to hear in utero and at birth, just as hearing-impaired humans feel the pulse of music through their skin.[6]

Although most dogs are able to filter out offensive sounds, others suffer from noise sensitivity disorders, developing fears and phobias to noises such as fireworks, thunder, and sirens. Household appliances that mean little to us in terms of sound can really hurt a dog's sensitive ears. Vacuum cleaners, roaring garbage trucks, or the cries of a baby cause misery for many dogs. I once worked with a dog that was terrified of going into the kitchen. To find out what was scaring him, I lay on the floor by the kitchen entrance, and as I did so, my ears picked up a low rumbling coming from my left. The air vent from the refrigerator emitted a deep hum that was almost undetectable at a human level but very loud from the dog's point of view. To test this theory, I turned the fridge off. Five minutes later the dog walked into the kitchen with no hesitation. When I took him out and turned the fridge back on again, he refused to go back in, even when presented with his favorite food as a lure. It was clear that the noise from the fridge was the culprit.

The Russian physiologist Ivan Pavlov discovered that dogs are so sensitive to tonal changes that they can detect even the most minute changes of pitch between two notes. With this in mind, I discovered that dogs can recognize certain types of music just as they recognize the sound of your car engine. I then discovered that there was another way to help dogs get over certain sound sensitivities and anxieties, by using music as part of a *sensory education* program. Working with the creators of Through a Dog's Ear, whose specially designed psycho-acoustic music helps to calm dogs in all environments ranging from the home to the shelter, I developed the Canine Noise Phobia Series, which pairs psycho-acoustic music and sound effects with a behavioral protocol designed to help a dog overcome sensitivities to certain sounds (see Resources). I have received very positive feedback about this series, which thankfully is now helping dogs overcome their fear of offending noises all over the world. (For more on its use, see chapter 7 on separation distress and anxiety and chapter 8 on thunderstorm phobia.)

SMELL

Although a dog's brain is just one-tenth the size of a human brain, the part of the brain that is devoted to analyzing smells is forty times greater than that of a human's. A dog's sense of smell is therefore estimated to be a hundred thousand times better than ours. Animal psychologist Alexandra Horowitz suggests that smell may be one way a dog perceives the passing of time. When a dog catches a scent on the air, it is seeing the future by smelling what is to come—and smelling odors on the ground is like scenting the past.[7]

The physiology of a dog's nose is incredible. According to animal psychologist Stanley Coren, a dog's nose print is as individual as a human's fingerprint.[8] Mobile nostrils that move independently from each other gather scent from all directions. Mucus on and inside the nose helps keep the nose skin or "leather" cool but also acts like sticky velcro, trapping scent molecules, which are then dissolved into the mucus and pushed up through the nose by tiny hairs called cilia. The average dog produces a pint of this mucus every day. When a dog sniffs, it disrupts its normal breathing process to gather scent. Sniffing prevents too much of the scent from being exhaled so that more of the scent can be identified. The nostrils lead to a bony shelflike structure where scent is trapped, and information gathered by receptor cells is then sent to the olfactory bulbs and on to the brain for processing.

"If a dog's sense of smell is so good, why do they smell each other's bottoms?" my daughter asked me one day. It was a fair question and one that I am often asked. Smelling the anogenital area of another animal may seem revolting, but this activity gives dogs plenty of information about the animal they are smelling. Dogs have what is known as a *vomeronasal organ*, which is located above the hard palate of the mouth just behind the incisors, at the base of the naval cavity. The information received through this organ goes straight to the part of the brain that processes emotional memory—the limbic system. It is believed that this organ helps detect *pheromones* (chemical messages that are produced by glands, urine, and feces).[9] Even though a dog's body is covered with glands, there is a large concentration of them in moist areas such as the anus, the ears, and around the mouth. A dog can tell the age, sex, reproductive status, and health of the recipient just by smelling these areas. It is also thought that dogs can detect changes of emotional state in other dogs and animals by smelling the concentration of stress chemicals in the secretions. For example, there is some truth to the belief that dogs can smell fear. Human sweat carries odors that change depending on the concentration of hormones in the body. When a person is stressed or fearful, adrenaline is released into the bloodstream, which elevates the heart rate and increases sweat production. A dog can easily detect when a human is stressed by the release of these chemicals along with body tension and shallow breathing.

When dogs urinate or defecate they are effectively marking their space and leaving behind information about themselves— the canine version of a business card or "pee-mail." When a dog rubs up against you, she may be doing it out of love and to get attention, but she may also be depositing her scent on you. Some dogs will go to great lengths to distribute their scent as far as possible by releasing spurts of urine at different times in different locations to cover a wider area. Sadie scrapes her back paws along the ground after she has toileted, spreading her scent by pushing it up into the air and leaving secretions on the ground from the glands located between her paw pads. I have seen many dogs literally doing handstands to get their urine as high as possible as well as dogs that poop up against walls or on raised surfaces such as a bush or mound of grass. After all, getting your message out at nose height makes it easier for others to read all about you.

As I mentioned earlier in this chapter, scent goes straight to the limbic system that regulates mood and drives emotions and memory. By using food when teaching, I am able to harness a dog's powerful sense of smell to help her learn and achieve emotional stability—an important part of sensory education. As I explained in chapter 2, food is an important part of the learning process and can help nervous and anxious dogs overcome their fears. Using other scents, such as synthetic dog-appeasing pheromone or lavender, helps lessen anxiety by promoting feelings of calm.[10] Putting a shirt with your scent on it in your dog's bed can help her cope during your absence. Encouraging your dog to learn by using scent work to improve her mental and physical state is a way of utilizing her sense of smell to encourage her to perform tasks that enrich her life and help her overcome any emotional issues she may have. If I'm working with a particularly nervous dog that is not responding to food, I warm up the food, releasing scent molecules and stimulating the digestive system. Even a fearful dog has a hard time resisting warmed-up hot dog.

Humans have long harnessed the dog's keen sense of smell by using them to search for and rescue people and to detect items as diverse as bombs, drugs, agricultural products, termites, mold, bedbugs, and accelerants. Because dogs process each smell separately (a skill known as odor layering), they can filter out other scents that might distract them from doing their job. Dogs are now being used to detect cancer, alert people with epilepsy to an impending seizure, and detect low and high blood sugar levels in diabetics.

A dog's sense of smell can be hampered by illness or old age or by being overheated and actively panting (because the dog is using its inhalations to cool itself rather than for detecting scents). These factors can reduce the sense of smell by as much as 40 percent. If your dog is cool, young, and healthy, though, her nose knows no bounds!

TASTE

Considering the way Sadie gulps down her food at every meal, I often wonder whether she can really taste anything. Taste and smell are closely linked, and although a dog's sense of smell is superior to ours, their tasting abilities are probably not as sensitive. A dog has only 1,700 taste buds, far fewer than the 9,000 taste buds we have.[11] Dogs can detect sweet, salty, sour, and bitter tastes, but it's doubtful they can discern subtle taste differences in food as easily as humans can.

Water is the only liquid I like drinking, and I have developed such a "taste" for it that I'm now extremely sensitive to changes in any water I drink. A dog's sense of taste for water lies on the tip of her tongue—the part that laps the water up. When a dog eats salty or sugary food, her sensitivity to the taste of water increases.[12] This ability may have evolved as a way of encouraging a dog to drink and keep hydrated while eating meat that is naturally high in salt. I like to believe that in respect to water, my taste is very much like a dog's.

Taste deterrents such as bitter apple or lemon are designed to prevent dogs from chewing things that they shouldn't. These substances are frequently put on furniture, walls, or whatever the dog is chewing in order to stop the behavior, but I've found that they often don't achieve the desired result. In my experience, some dogs actually *like* the taste of these substances, licking them off quickly to get to the other good stuff underneath. In this case I manage the situation by removing the object or preventing access.

TOUCH

As soon as a puppy is born, she relies on touch to find her mother, to stimulate milk flow for feeding, and as a source of comfort. Mothers in turn lick and nuzzle their puppies from birth, improving the puppies' circulation and encouraging them to eliminate waste in order to stay healthy. Touch helps form emotional bonds between a mom and her pups that can then be transferred to humans. It is really important that a puppy experience human touch from birth to promote a human/canine attachment and encourage the puppy's ability to develop social attachments with others as she grows.

If you look at your dog's face you will see that she has fine hairs or whiskers above the eyes, on the muzzle, and below the jaw on the side of the muzzle. These whiskers, or vibrissae, are so sensitive that when a dog approaches an object, she can sense changes in airflow long before she actually touches it. Because whiskers are so sensitive, take care when examining the inside of your dog's mouth or brushing her teeth, and don't buy into the whole practice of whisker trimming—those hairs are there for a reason.

Some dogs have an automatic defensive reflex to hands that come toward them or extend over their heads. This could be because the whiskers on top of the eyes itch or hurt when touched, but it's also possible that the dog views a hand stretching over her head as threatening. When a puppy is young, this reflex is not under conscious control, so it is vital to desensitize the puppy or dog to accept an approaching hand because this scenario is going to happen many times throughout life. (See Teaching the Touch Cue, page 60.) Touch sensitivities vary from dog to dog, but you should always use care when touching the head, muzzle, tail, abdomen, and paws.

Nerve endings along the dog's spine and toward the tail make the back a particularly sensitive area but one where most dogs like to be touched. Sadie enjoys scooting along the grass on her back, rubbing back and forth as she does so. The first few times I saw this I was concerned that she might be in pain, but thankfully it turns out that she just really enjoys a good back scratch.

A dog's paws are so sensitive they can detect different textures and vibrations in the ground. I remember seeing video of a dog suddenly freezing and bolting from a room. His owners were still wondering what had spooked him when, thirty seconds later, an earthquake struck. It was obvious that the dog had felt the vibrations in the ground long before his family had. Foot sensitivity is probably why so many dogs hate having their paws touched or nails clipped.

Habituating a pup to being touched from birth is extremely important as early pleasant experiences of human handling set a dog up for a lifetime of acceptance. Rubbing a nervous dog's chest in a circular motion can be very soothing, but if you want to go the extra mile, investing in a professional canine masseuse is a great way to help your dog relax.[13] Do this only if your dog likes being touched. For dogs that, like Niles, are stressed by too much handling, these therapies are not a good idea!

Be Mindful

As we learn more about what makes dogs tick, we can make their life experience better. Whenever I go into a home with a dog that is struggling to cope, I focus on finding ways to relieve some of the pressure she feels. Simple solutions, like placing the dog's bed in an area of low traffic or creating a denlike space or "safe zone" where she can take herself off for some peace and quiet, has huge benefits. Encouraging children to see the world from their dog's perspective helps them understand and appreciate their dog's life experience. By lowering expectations and accepting that dogs don't have to be sociable with everyone they meet, owners can better understand how to make their dogs feel more protected and secure. We don't necessarily want to say hello or be friendly to everyone we encounter, so why do we expect this of our dogs?

Allowing dogs to make autonomous decisions in certain situations relieves pressure and allows them to be more confident.

Guiding them slowly through situations that could otherwise be overwhelming and putting some structure into their day creates much-needed predictability, which is particularly beneficial for nervous dogs. Schedules are an easy way of making a day more predictable. As a nervous dog grows in confidence, schedules can slowly be varied until the dog is able to cope better with novelty in everyday situations.

Canine Emotion

There is still much debate about whether a dog's emotional experience is similar to that of a human's or whether a dog's behavior is simply influenced by an inner drive to survive. Although we do not yet have a definitive scientific answer to this question, science is helping us better understand how a dog's brain works. Scientific exploration is producing fascinating insights into dogs' emotional world. Some believe that although dogs have brains with the same basic structures and functions as ours, a dog's emotional experience is negligible. But just ask any dog owner whether their dog has emotions, and the answer is almost always an emphatic "Of course!"

Emotions are stimulated by biology and environment, creating physiological changes in our bodies. Falling in love with a person for the first time increases our heart rate, makes us perspire more, and causes butterflies in our stomach. We cry when we are sad and run away or fight when we are frightened. These are neurological, chemical, and hormonal changes that occur in response to environmental and situational stimuli. Feelings, however, are how we interpret these emotional experiences, so although we can say without a doubt that dogs do experience emotion, we can't yet be certain exactly how they *feel*. It's fascinating, however, to note the similarities in the internal and outward expression of emotions in both species.

It is an undisputed fact that emotions drive behavior by informing the brain what to do next and moving the dog (or human) toward comfort and pleasure or away from discomfort and pain. Emotion is filtered in the brain, and emotional significance is attached to new information by the amygdala. Emotionally loaded experiences are stored in the long-term memory, and the cortex or "thinking brain" applies social inhibition, impulse control, problem solving, and learning. Another area of the brain, the hypothalamus, regulates many of the body's functions and prepares the body's response to environmental and situational stimuli

Behavior is guided by a dog's life experiences and influenced by physiological processes, including the activity of neurotransmitters and hormones. *Neurotransmitters* such as serotonin and dopamine are electrical secretions that transmit chemical messages between neurons in the brains and bodies of dogs and humans; *hormones* are chemical messengers that travel through the bloodstream to the body's tissues and organs, affecting mood, metabolism, growth, and development. Because we share these mechanisms, humans and dogs have similar physiological reactions to emotional states such as joy, fear, and excitement. Serotonin, for example, has a profound effect on emotions and is responsible for regulating mood, enhancing positive feelings, and inhibiting aggressive responses. Dopamine helps to focus attention, promoting states of eagerness and purpose while creating feelings of satisfaction. A lack of these neurotransmitters causes irritability, limited impulse control, overreactivity, anxiety, and greater sensitivity to pain. Although these physiological reactions are similar in both species, the way in which emotions are processed in the brain could potentially be the key difference between the emotional experience of the two species. Human emotions flood through a cortex that is five times bigger than that of a dog, so a dog might have impressive cognitive abilities but processing emotion may be less complex because it is unadulterated by the human ability to analyze. Simply put, when a dog emotes, the feelings are probably very pure and not complicated by intricate human thought.

As I mentioned previously, a dog's nose dominates her brain, which is truly built around the information it gets from scent. Because smell is so closely linked to emotion, there is evidence that the dog's emotional experience might be even more intricate than we could imagine. Have you ever smelled something that evoked a positive or negative memory? Those memories are held with other emotionally loaded memories and can be "released" by a sensory trigger that alters your mood. Imagine having a dog's acute sense of smell and how intense the emotional memories and responses evoked as a result of a sensory trigger must be.

This knowledge provides us with crucial information about how the brain functions and how we can use the knowledge to help dogs learn and modify emotional states such as anxiety and fear. Stimulating a dog's sense of smell with food, for example, not only motivates a dog to learn but is also a valuable tool for changing the way a dog's brain works (see chapter 2, page 38).

As mentioned, dogs trained with compulsion and force suffer higher stress and anxiety than those trained using positive reward methods. When a dog is punished, cortisol is released into the bloodstream and readies the body for danger. When high levels of cortisol are released, the brain is overwhelmed and the resulting state interferes with rational thought. Stress from threat causes the dog to "shut down," effectively freezing her until the threat goes away. In this state of anxiety the dog ceases to learn and becomes more insecure, frightened, or angry. If she cannot practice avoidance, the only other option is to bite, which is why so many trainers and owners who use punitive techniques are bitten.

JEALOUSY

If dogs have similar emotional responses to humans, does that mean they are also capable of feeling jealous? If the definition of jealousy is "fear of rivalry; apprehension regarding the loss of another's exclusive devotion; distrustful watchfulness; vigilance in maintaining or guarding something,"[14] doesn't that perfectly describe what dogs appear to be feeling when they guard resources and space, monopolize an owner's attention, and fight with their "siblings"? According to veterinary behaviorists like Dr. Nicholas Dodman, director of animal behavior at Tufts University, dogs can be jealous and we shouldn't get too inventive in searching for other explanations when the obvious one is right in front of us.

Over the years, I have had many calls from clients asking for help because the dogs in their lives are exhibiting what seems to be jealous or "protective" behavior toward a family member. One example was a three-year-old male Pomeranian named Teddy Pom Pom. Teddy's owners, Martin and Mandy, had been married for seventeen years. Martin was a firefighter, and all he wanted after a tiring day at work was to come home and get into bed next to his lovely wife. But Teddy Pom Pom didn't think too highly of this intrusion and protected the bed and his mistress as if his life depended on it, biting Martin as he slipped under the covers. The scars on Martin's arms and legs were evidence of the many times that Teddy had successfully defended his territory and his mistress. Unbelievably, Mandy allowed this behavior to continue, making all kinds of excuses for her "baby's" behavior and eventually telling her husband to sleep in the guest room. Martin even joked that Mandy preferred this arrangement and suspected that Teddy was being used as the next greatest excuse to the headache: "Not tonight, dear—I have a dog."

I work with many dogs like Teddy Pom Pom that exhibit jealous or protective behavior by jumping between two embracing owners. In most cases, these dogs thrive on the attention they are given by the most important person in their life and do not appreciate another person or animal taking that attention away from them.

I showed Teddy that all good things came from Martin. Before entering the home, Martin picked up Teddy's favorite treats and toys that had been left outside the front door and gave them to him when he walked in. Martin did this each time he came home from work until Teddy finally made the association and began eagerly awaiting his return. When Martin left the house, so did Teddy's treats and toys, but they magically reappeared each time Martin came home.

Because Teddy behaved so badly in the bedroom, Mandy denied Teddy access to the bed (and to her) whenever he showed any signs of aggressive response. If Teddy so much as growled, he was placed on the floor and ignored. After ten seconds of calm, he was allowed onto the bed again and the scenario was repeated. Teddy could remain next to Mandy only if he calmly accepted Martin's presence, and because Teddy loved being next to her, it didn't take him long to catch on. I suspect Mandy was not as happy as Martin to see how quickly the removal technique worked, but even she had to admit that a contented dog and happy husband made life much easier for them all.

Because I am always teaching biting dogs to get off beds or sofas on my television show, I have apparently developed a false reputation as someone who believes dogs should never be allowed on any furniture. Actually, it's fine if your dog jumps onto the sofa or sleeps in bed with you. The only time I have an issue with dogs in beds or on sofas is when it results in negative or dangerous guarding behavior (or when a human sleeping partner is not on board with the decision to share the bed with Fido).

If you can't get near your partner because of a jealous dog, here's how to curb this behavior:

- If your dog tries to get between you and your partner while you are standing up and hugging, ignore her.
- If she tries to jump on you while you are hugging on the sofa, you and your partner should immediately stand up and ignore her.
- Don't look at, talk to, or touch your dog in either scenario.
- When she gets off the sofa, sit down again and wait for three to five seconds.
- If your dog keeps her four paws on the ground during that time, praise her.
- If she tries to jump up again during the praise, keep repeating the exercise until she has four on the floor or goes away.
- If your dog aggresses at your partner while being held in your arms or sitting on your lap, immediately put your dog on the floor and ignore.
- Once your dog is calm, pick her up and hold her again or put her back on your lap and repeat the exercise. Continue to place her on the floor, without contact, if she reacts negatively, but if she accepts your partner's closeness, praise and give her plenty of attention. Your partner can also reward your dog's compliance with your dog's favorite food or toy.

GUILT

Many owners tell me they're convinced that their dogs feel guilty after they have done something wrong. To feel guilt, however, an individual must have a certain level of self awareness, an understanding of how his or her behavior has affected others in the past, and a sense of how it will affect others in the future. We are brought up in a culture that teaches us to consciously feel guilty, ashamed, or embarrassed for things that we have done. Although dogs do have a degree of consciousness and are aware of the immediate consequences of their actions, it's not known if they are truly aware of how their behavior affects others. Because a dog's cerebral cortex is smaller than that of a human, it is believed that dogs do not have the capacity to generate something as complex as the self-consciousness needed to feel guilty or ashamed.[15]

When you tell your dog off for chewing something well after the act was committed, she may slink away or use deferential body signals in an attempt to appease your anger. Although your dog's behavior may look "guilty," is she offering those deferential signals because she truly feels guilt for what she has done, or is your anger causing the response? Psychologist Alexandra Horowitz designed a study to test whether the canine "guilty" look was really guilt (as defined in human terms) or an expression of deferential behaviors intended to appease an owner's anger. Horowitz asked an owner to leave her dog in a room with a piece of food after telling the dog not to eat it. Sometimes the food was left in view, sometimes the dog ate it, sometimes he left the food alone, and sometimes Horowitz removed the food herself but told the owner that her dog had eaten it. So when the food was gone, regardless of who had taken it, the owner naturally scolded the dog. Horowitz could thus observe that the actual guilt factor (whether or not the dog had eaten the food) did not change the frequency of the dog's seemingly guilty response. The dog behaved as if he were guilty, whether he had eaten the food or not, simply in response to the owner's body language and expression of anger.[16]

Humans are well aware of how they think and feel and how their behavior might affect others. This metacognition or self-awareness is linked to our reflective consciousness and is highly sophisticated. David Smith, PhD, a comparative psychologist at the University of Buffalo who has conducted extensive studies in animal cognition, reports growing evidence that animals such as dolphins and macaque monkeys share a human's ability to reflect, monitor, and regulate their own states of mind.[17] William Roberts and his team from the University of Western Ontario's Department of Psychology studied whether or not dogs could detect deceit and thus determine whether a person was being helpful or leading them astray. The study's results suggested that dogs relied heavily on human cues, rather than metacognitive ability, to learn whether someone was deceiving them.[18]

So in order to feel truly guilty, a dog must be mindful about the effect her behavior will have on others and know and care what others are thinking and feeling. Although the results of this research show that dogs probably don't have the capacity to feel guilt, what is great for all of us who love them is that studies like these are being done—studies that help advance our knowledge about the way dogs think and experience emotion.

Given the enormous advances in our understanding of what drives dogs to do what they do, it is no longer helpful or fair to devalue and dismiss a dog's emotional experience as being inferior to ours. Like humans, some dogs are more emotionally expressive than others, but that doesn't necessarily mean that if your dog is more reserved, she doesn't have the ability to feel. Knowing how emotionally driven dogs are, is it not more important than ever that we treat them with the respect they deserve? Dogs' emotional well-being is influenced by early experience just as much as ours is. Unstimulating or abusive environments, rough handling, and hard punishment can damage emotional growth because stress-related pathways in the brain are prevented from developing properly. Dogs with this kind of early experience don't make social attachments or cope with domestic life easily. I believe one of the reasons why humans and dogs have formed such a special relationship with each other is our mutual ability to express how we feel. We may not always understand each other, but at least we're trying, and the more we discover, the better our dogs' lives will be.

PART TWO

BEHAVIORAL TRAINING SOLUTIONS

5

THE POSITIVE PUPPY
Building a Solid Foundation

Elizabeth looked at me, bleary-eyed, while sipping a mug of hot coffee she had just made. At her feet lay a tiny white ball of fluff. "Don't let her fool you," she said. "The only reason she's sleeping now is because she's been up every night since we brought her home a week ago." Maggie, a nine-week-old Maltese puppy, was one of the cutest things I had ever seen, but Elizabeth's demeanor told a different story. "If someone had told me it was going to be this hard," she said, "I would never have chosen a puppy—this is worse than having a baby."

The arrival of a new puppy is indeed a life-changing event for everyone involved. One minute the puppy is curled up sleeping or playing with his littermates; the next, those littermates are gone, leaving him all alone in a new place. Some puppies adjust very quickly to a different environment, but others take much longer to settle. The first few weeks of life in a new home can be strange and frightening for a young dog, and while owners are coping with the life changes that accompany the arrival of a new pup, the puppy is also doing some pretty significant assimilating of his own.

I understood what Elizabeth was going through—like so many people who bring puppies into their lives, she was having a hard time adjusting. New parents fully expect to be kept awake at night with an infant but for some reason when the new addition is a puppy, the little one's nighttime needs are simply an irritant. I knew it wasn't going to be long before Maggie slept through the night, but I also knew that Elizabeth needed support. If she didn't get it, I feared she might do what tens of thousands of other puppy parents do each year and relinquish Maggie to the shelter. Elizabeth had a lot of work ahead of her because raising a puppy properly is no easy task. Those first developmental weeks are crucial, and I wanted to make sure that everything possible would be done to ensure that Maggie's mental and physical health was as sound as it could be. The next couple of weeks would have a big impact on her future success or failure in adapting to human domestic life.

The best time to bring a new puppy or dog into your home is when at least one member of your family has time to spend with the puppy during the adjustment period, which can last up to two weeks or more. It's not advisable to get a new dog if all of the members in your family are out of the house all day during the transition period. Conversely, I do *not* recommend you remain beside your puppy during his every waking moment. You can achieve a happy medium by allowing your puppy to investigate, explore, and experience his new home, giving him plenty of attention while also giving him the space he needs to adjust to his new surroundings. By gradually exposing him to being away from his mother and siblings, you will set him up to better cope when you eventually leave him on his own for longer periods.

Maggie slept in a crate in Elizabeth's room, but because the crate was some distance from the bed, she spent most of the night whimpering and crying for attention. The first couple of weeks can be the loneliest for a pup, so I moved her crate close to Elizabeth's bed and added a soft toy so that Maggie had something to cuddle up to. Some people prefer their puppy to sleep in bed with them, which is fine as long as the pup's nighttime toileting needs are taken care of and all other bedmates are okay with this arrangement. The first few weeks of nighttime potty outings were exhausting for Elizabeth, but the sleep interruptions gradually decreased as Maggie built up bladder control and began to sleep through the night. Elizabeth was then able to move the crate farther from the bed to a permanent sleeping area. The longer Maggie slept through the night, the more active she became during the day, but like most young puppies she still needed a lot of sleep and was allowed to take naps as needed. Puppies are easily exhausted from taking in so much new information.

The Importance of Positive Socialization, Habituation, and Enrichment

Society dictates that our dogs must be well-mannered in our homes and in public, which puts a great deal of pressure on dogs as well as owners. It's very common for a young puppy to experience emotional changes as he grows, but providing him with a good foundation from the beginning will help you deal with any unforeseen challenges that may come your way. The time you invest at the beginning of your puppy's life will allow him to become a confident and well-adjusted adult. Most dogs cope well living in a human world, but few people realize just how resilient a pet has to be to conform to the rules that domestic life imposes on them. Sadly, failure to follow these rules results in many of them ending up in shelters.

We want our dogs to be friendly and well mannered with everyone they meet in and out of the home, even if socializing makes them feel uncomfortable. Although we have the freedom to choose who we want to greet and who to avoid, our dogs almost never have that luxury. Some people just do not understand how threatening and uncomfortable it is for some dogs when their personal space is invaded by a stranger. Of course, because we desire and expect our dogs to be adaptable and emotionally stable at all times (high expectations that even we humans can't live up to) when they react negatively to "friendly" human interaction, they are punished for antisocial behavior.

Because puppies are not born social animals—that is, instinctively welcoming and freely associating with humans, strange dogs, and other animals—they have to learn to bond with others through early positive experience. Socialization, whereby puppies and dogs are exposed to different environments and social stimuli, is crucial in promoting confidence. The sensitive time for socialization is approximately four to twelve weeks of age, and puppies between the ages of eight and ten weeks often experience what is known as the "fear period." Any negative life experiences that occur during this period can make a lasting impression for the rest of a dog's life.

Positive socialization teaches dogs important social skills and helps them grow up with confidence. Overexposing a puppy, however, may have the opposite effect—a dog that hates being touched and fears other dogs and humans. Socializing a puppy correctly can make the difference between an adaptable dog that copes well in various situations and one that will never function well in society. This is one of the many reasons why puppies bred in puppy mills and sold over the Internet or in pet stores tend to have so many behavioral issues. Unfortunately, the common experience for these puppies consists of impersonal rearing in a socially deprived environment with no positive human interaction, followed by premature separation from the mother and littermates and then a traumatic trip to the pet store—all occurring during the time when good social experiences are critical.

Dr. Andrew Luescher, animal behaviorist and director of the Animal Behavior Clinic at Purdue University, has found that deficiencies in early development can have adverse effects on a dog's behavior and disposition. He explains that puppies are more balanced temperament-wise when they remain with their mothers until they are seven to eight weeks old; puppies taken away from their mothers too soon are more likely to be fearful, hyperactive, or even fear-aggressive (feeling fearful of a perceived threat can lead to an aggressive response as a means of self-defense).[1] This is because early and enriching experiences help the brain develop normally. To optimize your puppy's social skills, good things must happen when people meet him for the first time. Introductions to other puppies and adult dogs must be made in a calm manner so as not to overwhelm.

We took Maggie to a puppy play group where she could learn important social skills and made sure that the other puppies in the group were matched in size and temperament. We taught her basic learning skills and cues at home and also practiced these cues in a class environment, so she learned to pay attention to Elizabeth even when distracted. Some classes won't take puppies until their vaccinations are complete, while others take pups as young as ten weeks old—the prime time for socialization. We monitored Maggie's interactions with the other pups to guard against negative experiences.

If you can't find an appropriate puppy class in your area, there are other ways to give your pup new experiences. Finding a friend for a play date or taking your puppy on a car ride will allow him to experience an outside environment, even if he has to be in your arms until it is safe for him to walk in public.

A puppy tends to have a short attention span, so be sure to take regular breaks while teaching. Even older dogs need frequent breaks to process what they have learned, perfecting it later through repetition. Every dog is different, so watch yours carefully: if he begins to avoid contact with other dogs, lies down, or gets snappy at another dog's approach, give him some time away from the situation.

As soon as Maggie came into the home, Elizabeth began to habituate her to the various experiences she was likely to encounter in her life, including being handled by us, the veterinarian, and the groomer. I was careful not to bombard Maggie with constant touching by too many strangers but allowed her to habituate gently. Touch-sensitive areas such as the mouth, paws, tail, and belly were handled very carefully so that Maggie wouldn't find having her teeth checked or nails trimmed unpleasant in the future. I rewarded her acceptance and calm behavior with praise, treats, and toys that she liked, making sure that the rewards were only given when she was content.

Maggie was introduced to many different environmental and situational experiences including riding in the car, meeting people, and playing at the vet's office. The more positive interactions she had, the more resilient her brain became and the better she coped with novel experiences and situations. These positive experiences affect brain growth by encouraging connections to develop between neurons in the brain; the more varied the experience, the more the physiology of the brain is shaped appropriately. The thicker the dog's cerebral cortex, the higher the concentration of vital brain enzymes associated with transmission of information to and from various parts of the brain will be. This not only helps a dog learn but also gives him the ability to solve problems and control impulses in domestic situations without being prompted. Socialization creates a more socially acceptable dog.[2]

Although we encouraged Maggie to follow Elizabeth around (a good foundation for teaching the "come" cue), we also made sure there were times when she was separated from Elizabeth in the house. Independence training in the home teaches a puppy to cope without you when you are away. Separation anxiety is not fun for dogs or owners and is a very difficult condition to treat, so set your puppy up for success from the beginning by teaching him to be emotionally secure without you. (For more on separation anxiety, see chapter 7.)

Puppy Mouthing

Pups like Maggie like to explore the world with their mouths, and everything is a potential chew toy. Providing a safe home environment to prevent inappropriate chewing on household items and teaching your puppy bite inhibition from an early age will help protect him and others as he grows. I taught Maggie that any mouthing or nipping a person's skin or clothes stopped play and attention immediately. When she nipped at me or Elizabeth, we got up and walked out of the room. We remained outside for a minute and then came back to resume play and attention. If she mouthed again, play stopped, but if she kept her teeth to herself, the game and attention continued. We gave her toys to keep her entertained and to use as distractions if needed, which helped redirect her mouthing to something more appropriate. I told Elizabeth to expect a second chewing phase when Maggie went through the first stages of adolescence between six to nine months of age.

Building a Common Language

It's never too early to teach your puppy cues such as "sit" and "come" that you can use to build a common language between you. A good recall cue is vital for the safety of your puppy or dog in all environments, and the sooner you start teaching it, the more reliable it will be. (I will cover other valuable cues later in the book.)

THE RECALL CUE

Most puppies will "come" to you whenever you decide to walk away because they instinctively like to follow you. Instilling a reliable response, however, usually takes months of consistency and positive reinforcement. The easiest way to teach your new puppy or dog the "come" cue is to begin using it as soon as you bring them home:

- Whenever your puppy or dog is coming to you on his own, wait until he is a couple of feet from you and then say his name and the word "come."
- When he gets to you, make a big fuss over him.
- With this exercise, your dog will learn that coming to you is a really good thing. After a while, you can lengthen the distance between you before you say the cue word, but be careful that you don't go too far too soon.
- If you want a reliable recall, do not chase your dog unless it is an emergency. Dogs love to be chased.
- If you call your dog a number of times and he doesn't come back to you, don't tell him off when he eventually returns. It is understandably annoying when your dog ignores you, but if he comes back only to find that you're angry with him, he'll actually learn to avoid you more. He won't understand that you're angry because he ignored you and will

think you're annoyed because he came back. Coming to you should always be rewarded, whatever the circumstance and no matter how long it took him to respond.

- Motivate your dog to come by being excited, running away from him, waving a toy, or having delicious food for him when he gets to you. This will instill the idea that coming back to you is the best thing he can ever do.

THE SIT CUE

Teaching your puppy or dog to "sit" gives both of you an action cue on which to build a common language and helps to teach valuable impulse control. This "safety" cue can be used when you need your puppy or dog to focus his attention at specific times (for example, at the curb before crossing the road, in front of a food bowl before eating, at the front door when someone is coming in, and before the leash is attached). As with any cue, teach this in short steps so that your puppy doesn't get bored, and be aware of your pup or dog's physical comfort. Sitting too much can be uncomfortable, especially for larger dogs.

- Hold a treat by your dog's nose and wait for him to figure out how he is going to get it out of your hand. Some dogs will lick or paw at it, but don't give it to him until he puts his behind on the floor.
- Repeat this until your dog is sitting reliably, then add the word "sit" as he is in the process of sitting so that he begins to associate the word with the action.
- When he is sitting repeatedly, start saying the word "sit" as you present the treat to him, and your dog will respond.
- Please note that if your dog is snappy or aggressive around food, you should be very careful and substitute a toy for the

food. Using toys to teach this instead of food is also effective if your dog is more toy motivated.

Adolescence

Just like human kids, puppies can sometimes be difficult to handle during adolescence, which for most dogs is around six to eighteen months of age. A puppy that once came when called may now develop an acute case of selective hearing, choosing to come only when he wants to. Puppy play can turn into pushy behavior that offends other dogs, causing disagreements and fights. Adult dogs that are normally tolerant of young pups will suddenly show their objections to rude behavior, and the pup that used to back down from a warning may now choose to stand his ground. This is the time when the young dog begins to test his human family as well as other dogs he meets, and it's why so many adolescent dogs end up in shelters; people are put off by this change in behavior.

Bearing this change in mind, early learning is even more important and provides a solid foundation so that when adolescence rears its sometimes ugly head, communication is clear and boundaries have been set. You may find that you have to put in extra time with your dog and watch his interactions with others a lot more closely so that you can stop a situation before it gets out of hand. In adolescence, dogs tend to be more fearful or shy than they were as puppies. It amazes me how closely these behavioral phases mirror what we humans experience, except that, thanks to dog years, theirs seems to come much earlier. Adolescence doesn't last long, but many people are greatly relieved when this phase of a dog's life is over.

General Puppy-Teaching Tips

- Start teaching in an environment free from distractions, such as a quiet room in your home, before teaching outside in your yard or in the park. Puppies and adult dogs learn faster when there is less around to distract them. Once your puppy is responding well in one environment, gradually introduce him to others. Don't always teach in the same place. Use all the rooms in your home as well as your yard, street, car, and local park. This ensures that your puppy learns to respond in varied environments and not just in one place.
- When teaching a new cue, keep sessions short to prevent boredom.
- Three five-to-ten-minute teaching sessions a day are recommended for teaching new cues, but communication and behavioral exercises should be rehearsed throughout daily life.
- Tired pups don't learn. Remember that mental activity can be more exhausting than physical activity.
- Use a mixture of vocal and physical communication.
- Vary the position of your body and distance while teaching action cues such as "sit" and "stay."
- Teaching should be as fun as playing. Puppies get bored easily, so be energetic and interesting.
- Be consistent—pups love predictability.
- Be patient and don't be afraid of failure.
- Reinforce good behavior throughout your dog's life.
- Try to prevent emotional highs and lows.
- Never use punishment or try to dominate your puppy or dog. This will damage the relationship between you and exacerbate aggressive response.
- Make it easy for your pup to do well.

pup's environment to avoid sensory deprivation.

nty of puppy-appropriate toys to play with.

s should end on a good note with plenty of praise.

d help teaching your puppy or dog and are unsure how to deal with a problem behavior, hire a trainer to help you. Avoid trainers that recommend choke, prong, or shock collars, and make sure that your trainer uses humane positive reinforce ment methods only. (To find a Victoria Stilwell Positively Dog Trainer in your area, go to www.positively.com/trainers.)

6

HOUSETRAINING HELL
Solving Toileting Issues

Roxy and Rio were eight-month-old Greyhound sisters that had the worst toileting issues I had ever seen. They belonged to a young couple who had never raised puppies before and thought that over time their dogs would learn to toilet outside by themselves and the messing in the home would stop. Six months later, the couple was still cleaning up mounds of poop and puddles of urine three times a day, every day. The smell of urine overwhelmed me as I entered the dogs' main toileting area. Roxy and Rio were charming, happy dogs, but as they came to greet me and jumped up to say hello, I felt a warm splash of urine on my face. This was going to be a long day.

Successful Housetraining

Toileting "accidents" are some of the most common issues I encounter, driving owners to the point of insanity and dogs into confinement. Usually this issue is resolved relatively quickly by helping a young pup learn how to eliminate appropriately, but occasionally older dogs develop behavior issues that negatively affect their ability to potty properly. Toileting is obviously a necessary act that removes harmful waste from the body, but the number of dogs that are given up by their families and surrendered to rescue shelters because of toileting problems is far too high.

Having gone through the process of housetraining Jasmine when she was a puppy (see chapter 10), I realize how fixated I became on her toileting habits. Elimination is closely linked to physical and emotional health. When a previously housetrained dog begins to toilet inappropriately, I always begin with an investigation into the dog's physical condition.

Successful housetraining is one of the first things the owner of a new puppy or dog needs to accomplish, and even though the learning process can be time consuming, it doesn't have to be daunting. By employing a combination of consistency, common sense, and positive reinforcement protocols, you can quickly train any dog to toilet appropriately. Housetraining is also an invaluable building block that helps dogs and people better understand one another while developing a personalized communication process. This understanding creates a strong bond based on mutual trust and respect, ensuring both parties enjoy a healthy relationship.

Toilet Training: Getting Started

Before starting the housetraining process, understand that from the perspective of new puppies or untrained dogs, there is no good reason in their minds why they should not toilet inside the home. It is up to people to give their dogs the tools they need to succeed in a domestic world, and that starts with helping them learn where it is appropriate to toilet. There are a number of ways to toilet train a dog successfully; your choice really depends on the type of environment you live in. People in urban living

situations with no yard tend to paper train the
the pups have had all their vaccinations at appro
weeks old. When it is safe for the puppy to be ou
the transition between paper training inside a
side. In contrast, those in suburban or rural environments with
yards or a safe outside area might use a combination of training
pads and outside toileting, while others skip pads altogether and
take their pups straight outside.

PAPER-TRAINING GUIDELINES

- Create a "safe zone" area where the puppy can be confined
  when unsupervised. This can be either a pen or a small
  puppy-proofed room with the pup's bed or crate, food, and
  water bowl.
- Line the entire area with training pads. At first the puppy
  will toilet all over the place, but this way it will always be on
  a pad.
- Remove soiled pads frequently.
- Reduce the number of pads by taking away one pad every
  few days, leaving a small area without a pad. Because the
  puppy has built up a habit of toileting on the pads, she should
  naturally gravitate to the area where the pads are still covering the floor, leaving the unpadded area clean.
- Puppies instinctively do not like to toilet too near where they
  eat or sleep, so ensure that the first pads you remove are the
  ones closest to the pup's bed and bowls.
- Over the next few weeks, gradually reduce the toileting
  area by removing each pad until there is one single pad left.
  Ensure that the remaining pad is the farthest from pup's bed
  and bowl, and change any soiled pads regularly.

- Use a cue word ("go potty," for example) that the puppy will associate with toileting, and quietly say that word while she is in the act of toileting. When she has finished, gently praise her and/or give her a favorite treat or toy as a reward. Repeating this process consistently will build up an association between the word and the act of toileting so that you can use the word to encourage the puppy to toilet.

- If the puppy is making the transition from toileting on pads inside to going outside, take a partially soiled pad to an appropriate outside area and place it on the ground. This will encourage the puppy to toilet outside while still having the comforting feel of the pad underneath her paws.

- Once the puppy is confident about going outside, remove the use of indoor pads completely.

- If you want to designate a permanent toileting area in your home, make sure you choose a quiet area. As you give your puppy more freedom, encourage her to use the pad by leading her to this area at hourly intervals and then less frequently as she learns to hold herself for longer periods.

- The puppy should now be at the stage where she is taking herself to her pad to toilet.

Be especially vigilant and prepared for a dog to eliminate at the following times:

- Immediately after meals
- After training sessions
- Shortly after waking
- After vigorous play
- During or after a stressful event
- When overly excited

WHAT *NOT* TO DO

Never scold a dog for toileting inappropriately, and never rub her nose in or near her mess. Contrary to popular opinion, a puppy or dog does not toilet inappropriately out of spite. If you catch your puppy or dog in the act of toileting in the home, issue a gentle vocal interrupter (I use "uh-oh") and pick her bottom off the ground. Remove her to the pad or outside and encourage her to toilet in that area. If a puppy is punished for toileting, the punisher becomes someone to be feared, and the pup will then be inclined to either toilet in secret or hold herself until the person is out of sight. This does not bode well for those who want their dogs to toilet when out on a walk! Leaving poorly housetrained puppies or dogs in the home unsupervised sets them up to fail unless they are in a "safe area."

THE ROLE OF THE CRATE

Crate training is a popular way of encouraging puppies to hold themselves for longer periods of time and of keeping them safe when unsupervised. Used correctly, a crate encloses a puppy safely and becomes a favorite place for sleeping and/or quiet time. But keeping a puppy or a dog in a crate for too long can also inadvertently encourage the dog to toilet where she sleeps, increasing the potential for anxiety problems to develop. If you use the crate correctly, it can be a highly effective toilet training tool as well as a comfortable den.

Some puppies love their crates; others need a bit of time to acclimate. When we first brought our nervy little rescue pup, Jasmine, home with us, she took to her crate almost immediately, most likely because she recognized it as a safe, quiet place in her strange new house. When I introduce a puppy to the crate, I make it comfortable with bedding and safe toys and leave the door open so that the puppy can investigate, while encouraging her to go in by throwing a favorite treat or chew inside. If the puppy decides to settle, I allow her to do so without closing the door so that she can make her own decision about whether to stay or leave. Once she is comfortable in the crate, I begin closing the door for a few seconds at a time, gradually building up the duration as long she is relaxed.

At this stage I like to give the puppy a durable rubber chew toy with some food inside so that she has the pleasure of chewing and eating while she is in the crate. Then I gradually increase the distance between myself and the crate until I can go about my own business while the puppy is settled. This process can take a few hours to a few days, but it's important not to rush. If the puppy begins to whine or bark, I wait until she is quiet before opening the door to let her out.

Each time puppy goes into her crate, I pair that decision with a cue such as "go to bed." This builds up an association between the cue and the action of walking into the crate so that she knows what to do when she hears those words in the future. Building up a positive association with puppy's crate means I can travel with my pup more successfully. This whole process can be used to help adult dogs acclimate to a crate too, but remember that some dogs do not adjust well to being confined in this way and do better in a pen or a safe room in your home.

TOILET-TRAINING SCHEDULES

As with most teaching, successful toilet training depends on consistency and repetition. Creating a recurring schedule that everyone in your household follows is crucial to helping your dog learn what is appropriate and what is not. Here is a typical schedule that I use to toilet train puppies; this is only a general guide and can be changed to fit specific needs.

7:30 **8 a.m.:** Take the puppy out to toilet as soon as you wake up.

8:00 **8:30 a.m.:** Feed the puppy the first meal of the day. Leave the food down for twenty minutes; after that time, pick up any that remains. Take the puppy outside immediately after eating and give her time to toilet again. *8:20*

8:30 **9 a.m.:** Puppy can now have supervised free time in the home as long as she has toileted.

8:45 **9:30 a.m.:** Take the puppy to her crate or the "safe zone" for an unsupervised nap or some play time.

9:45 **10:30 a.m.:** Take the puppy out to toilet again. WALK

Noon: If the puppy is eating three meals a day, feed her at this time. When she is six months old you can reduce feeding to twice a day. Leave the food down for twenty minutes and pick up what is left. Take her out to toilet immediately after feeding.

12:30–2:30 p.m.: Puppy goes into her crate or to the safe zone for a nap, play, or chew time.

2:30 p.m.: Take the puppy out to toilet.

3 to 5 p.m.: Give the puppy half an hour of full supervised home access only after she has toileted and follow that with unsupervised time in the crate or safe zone.

6 p.m.: Give the puppy the last daily feeding. Leave the food down for twenty minutes and remove any food that remains. Take puppy out immediately after feeding to toilet. WALK

6 p.m. till bedtime: Use a mixture of crate and safe zone time, supervised free time in the home, and/or access to outside for toilet breaks.

As your puppy grows, you will find that you don't need to take her out as often. As a general rule, puppies at rest can hold themselves for up to one hour for every month of age. Vigorous play or other stimulation can reduce this time. Crate time can happen throughout the day, but it shouldn't last longer than your puppy can cope with, which will depend on your puppy's age and the progress she is making. Keeping a pup in a crate for too long causes accidents, inappropriate chewing, and anxiety.

I used all of the preceding protocols with Roxy and Rio, and within two weeks of my visit there had been significant improvement. After six weeks with no accidents in the home, their exhausted but happy owners finally declared their dogs housetrained.

Toileting Issues

One of the most irritating behaviors that dog owners complain about is that even if their dogs seem to be well housetrained, they still urinate inside. In some cases this elimination is attributed to dogs' desire to mark territory; in others, urination and defecation are seen as an expression of anxiety or an inability to hold themselves when excited.

SCENT MARKING

Joel and Eileen had two female and two male Chihuahuas with a serious scent-marking problem that had rotted the wooden floors in the dining room where the dogs spent most of their time. The entire house smelled of urine. By the time I arrived, the couple had effectively given up, noting that while stopping one dog from scent marking was a tough task, stopping all four seemed to be impossible. The dogs had ample opportunity to go outside, but competition among the four meant that as far as they were concerned their food, bedding, chair legs, and other objects existed merely to be marked on a daily basis. The situation had become desperate for the family, but the solutions were actually quite simple and easily workable.

Scent marking is a very normal and common behavior (particularly in male dogs), but it becomes a big problem when marking occurs in the home. As mentioned in chapter 4, dogs mark to advertise their presence or to claim territory and resources. Pheromones in urine and feces play a large part in canine communication, containing chemical messages that pass along valuable information about the marker, such as age, sex, health, and reproductive status. These pheromones are concentrated in the moist areas of a dog's body, including the anogenital region, the ears, and the mouth. Glands are also contained within every hair follicle on a dog's body. Urination has a competitive component but can also occur if a dog is overstimulated during or after vigorous play, or if a dog becomes anxious in a particular situation (such as when a person leaves). This common expression of anxiety is often mistaken for spite, resulting in punishment, which only increases the behavior.

Both sexes scent mark, but unneutered males are the worst offenders because the presence of testosterone stimulates signaling of sexual availability and claiming of territory. In many cases, neutering can significantly reduce the desire to scent mark, but some dogs continue even after they have been "fixed." Resources such as toys, food bowls, chew treats, bones, and beds are the most likely objects to be marked, and in some cases a dog will actually mark a person or something that smells heavily of that person, such as a sofa or bed. Scent marking is usually more common in multidog households where dogs compete for space, resources, and human attention.

Although this can be a difficult behavior to work with, scent marking can be tackled successfully by taking the following steps:

- Remove high-value resources such as bones and food bowls that encourage competitive marking.
- Do not allow the dog or dogs that scent mark to roam freely around the home.

- To prevent access to favorite marking spots during times when you are unable to actively supervise your dogs, confine them to a dog-proofed room or crate.
- Avoid competitive or vigorous play indoors, as excess activity encourages urination.
- If a dog is about to mark, interrupt the behavior with a vocal interrupter and immediately direct the dog to something more positive or take her outside.
- Help a marking dog succeed by taking her to new and different areas on walks. This will encourage her to mark outside rather than in the home, but take care not to allow your dog to toilet in neighbors' yards and please be considerate by picking up any poop!

The four Chihuahuas' desire to scent mark was eliminated by using the methods listed. I often find that boredom and lack of mental stimulation and physical exercise exacerbates marking behavior, so a daily schedule of activities that kept the dogs occupied, along with good environmental management, was the perfect prescription for happier dogs and a cleaner household.

EXCITABLE OR SUBMISSIVE URINATION

Dogs that urinate when excited or nervous should never be scolded. Elimination can be an expression of anxiety, and punishment only makes this issue worse. In these cases, each new person who comes into the home must give limited attention to the dog until she is calm. When attention is finally given, the person should resist approaching the dog and allow her to make her own decision whether she wants to greet, relieving social pressure and curbing the need to release urine from stress.

HOUSETRAINING OLDER DOGS

Teaching older dogs that have not previously been taught to toilet appropriately can also be a challenge. Most dogs raised in a normal domestic environment respond well to a good housetraining schedule, but those that have lived in puppy mills are notoriously difficult to teach. Dogs prefer not to toilet where they sleep and eat, but because of cramped conditions, puppy-mill dogs are forced to do just that. Transitioning from a puppy mill into a home can therefore be problematic and makes crate training—usually a successfully way to toilet train a dog—much less effective. However, even puppy mill dogs can be taught to toilet appropriately with a good schedule that goes back to basics, allowing access to outside areas every hour, encouraging the dog to toilet with a verbal cue, and then gradually decreasing the frequency of trips as the dog builds up control. Following a schedule builds up a ritual of behavior that eventually becomes predictable and reliable. Human patience and sensitivity is the key to success, especially when dealing with dogs with compromised backgrounds like puppy-mill survivors.

There is no doubt that housetraining issues cause a great deal of distress for owners and their dogs, but any toileting issue can be solved relatively quickly with patience and understanding. Toileting is closely linked to physical and mental health, so if you are concerned about your dog's toileting habits, pay a visit to your veterinarian, who can rule out any medical issues your dog may have before you start on a schedule or modification plan.

7

HOME-ALONE BLUES

Easing Separation Distress and Anxiety

Dogs and humans have a natural, mutual need to form social attachments—a need that results in our rare and shared ability to develop close relationships with species other than our own. Most dogs thrive in social groups, forming strong bonds with the families with which they live. Although some dogs may not particularly like being left alone, most learn to cope with their owner's absence. Some dogs, however, become so distressed when their families leave that they experience the canine version of a panic attack, resulting in excessive vocalization, pacing, whining, panting, inappropriate toileting, and destructiveness. These dogs are desperate to reestablish contact with their owners. I have worked on cases where dogs have jumped out of windows or chewed through doors in a desperate attempt to find their families, causing major destruction and injury to both their homes and themselves. It's not only upsetting for the families whose dogs suffer such distress but also endlessly exasperating for them to return to a half-eaten wall or a broken window.

Dogs that suffer from separation distress and anxiety are often hypervigilant even when their owners are home, following them from room to room and growing increasingly anxious when the time comes for them to leave. Some of these behaviors can be relatively mild to begin with, but in my experience, if ignored at this stage, these issues can easily escalate into a more serious anxiety-related condition. Separation distress and anxiety has many causes, but genetics, trauma, removing pups from their mother and littermates too soon (before seven weeks), and an early history of abandonment can contribute to what quickly becomes a deeply rooted problem that is highly resistant to change. Any breed of dog can develop this debilitating condition at any age, and its sudden onset in older dogs suggests that this anxiety is also linked to cognitive decline.

It seems that the number of separation anxiety cases is on the rise, probably due largely to societal changes in domestic situations. As more people leave the house to work elsewhere, animals are spending longer hours at home by themselves with nothing to do. Some dogs spend their whole lives waiting for their people to come home, with few opportunities to socialize or any outlets to relieve their boredom and anxiety throughout the day. These dogs feel a desperate relief when their owners come home and a rising panic when they leave again. The resulting physical and material destruction is hard to come home to, which is why so many dogs with separation issues unfortunately end up in shelters.

Boredom Equals Mischief

Coming home to a mangled sofa or half-eaten wall does not necessarily mean your dog is suffering from separation distress. In many cases this destruction is simply the result of boredom. When clients tell me their dogs have separation problems, I'm always careful to first establish whether the issues their dogs have are anxiety-based because making assumptions about behavior without concrete evidence can mean a lot of wasted time and energy dealing with a problem that doesn't really exist.

Hoss, a four-year-old rescued male Weimaraner, had previously been "rehomed" many times due to his destructive behavior. He was a strong, powerful dog capable of doing great damage if not crated during his owner's absence, and his chosen area of destruction in his new home was mainly centered in the kitchen and by the front door. Neighbors reported barking coming from inside the house when the owners were away. As a result, Hoss and the three dogs he lived with were never left by themselves for fear of the damage they would do.

I wanted to get an accurate picture of Hoss's behavior so I could see for myself whether the destruction was indeed a result of the distress his family thought he was experiencing when they left him. To do this, I set up video cameras in areas of the home where the destruction was historically the worst and then left the house with the family. When we returned an hour later, the home looked like it had been hit by a tornado, but the dogs themselves acted as if nothing had happened. Little did Hoss know that we had been spying on his every move.

I love watching what dogs do when they are home alone, and Hoss's antics were particularly entertaining. The big Weimaraner stood by the front door, waiting for us to get into the car and pull out of the driveway. Once he was satisfied we had gone, he walked into the kitchen. With one paw he opened a drawer and investigated the contents inside, pulling out a couple of kitchen towels and taking them off into the sitting room where the other dogs were patiently waiting. After some fun chew time, Hoss casually sauntered back into the kitchen and, resting one paw on the top of the kitchen counter, used the other to open the top cabinet. In one swift motion he knocked a jar of peanut butter out of the cabinet and onto the counter, took it into his mouth, and carried it off into the sitting room. The other dogs in the household, having grown tired of chewing on boring kitchen towels, took advantage of the opened drawer and removed other bits and pieces to play with. Only ten minutes had passed, and the house already looked like there had been a burglary. Hoss then proceeded to chew through the plastic peanut butter jar and eat the contents. After his feast, he walked around to see whether there was anything else to steal before contentedly wandering to his bed to fall asleep. Back in the living room, the other dogs were still chewing on various kitchen utensils, while a new dog the family was fostering paced up and down by the front door, barking. Half an hour later, all the dogs—having enjoyed themselves immensely—fell asleep and remained that way until we returned.

Destruction that occurs when dogs are by themselves can indeed be attributed to separation distress, especially when focused on exit points such as doors and windows, but it was very clear from the video footage I filmed over several days that even though Hoss may have suffered from separation-related issues in the past, living in a home with other dogs had turned anxiety into mischief. Boredom and lack of appropriate physical exercise and mental stimulation was the cause of Hoss's destructive behavior. Weimaraners are an energetic breed, so with no outlet to release his energy, Hoss had decided to use his excellent problem-solving and hunting skills to find jars of peanut butter, which made his owners' absences very appealing. I could almost see the gleam in his eye when he saw we were leaving.

I recommended that the family exercise their dogs daily, including playing retrieval games in the backyard. It's very important to give certain breeds an opportunity to do what they were bred to do: pointing, flushing, and retrieving duck-scented dummies gave Hoss an engaging new outlet to channel his physical and mental energy. He was given further mental stimulation by learning new action cues that centered on impulse control and problem solving, such as "sit," "stay," "wait," and "leave it." I advised the family manage their environment and block access to the kitchen area when the dogs were alone as well as provide them with appropriate activity toys to play with. These small changes made a world of difference in all the dogs' lives, and Hoss never felt the need to steal again.

Exercise and Environmental Enrichment

The world is full of unemployed dogs! Enriching your dog's life experience reduces boredom, anxiety, and other behavioral issues that can arise when he might otherwise have nothing to do.

Taking your dog on at least one long daily walk is essential for his physical and mental health. Exercise is a potent stress reliever for all animals, so a good walk not only exercises a dog physically but also provides a different environment to challenge and stimulate his senses. Unlike feral dogs, the domesticated dog lives in a sensory-deprived environment, which in many cases causes big problems. A regular walk schedule will enhance your dog's life immeasurably by increasing levels of serotonin, which plays an important role in lowering stress and controlling undesirable impulsive behavior. Inactivity contributes to destructive behaviors such as chewing, inappropriate toileting, excessive barking, and other anxiety-based behaviors such as separation anxiety and aggression. Dogs that are regularly left alone for long hours shouldn't be blamed for taking out their boredom and loneliness on the couch. Chewing gives a dog something to do and triggers the release of pleasurable endorphins into the body, which modulates stress and gives the dog a feeling of comfort and well-being.

I am constantly surprised by clients who complain about their dogs' destructive behavior yet fail to give them regular exercise. It's an alien concept to me, because personally I don't feel right each day until I've taken my dogs out for a good long walk. I make time for them even if my schedule is busy, because not doing so prevents them from doing what dogs are really good at—scenting, investigating, socializing, and having some well-earned freedom.

A former client of mine bred and showed Maltese—beautiful dogs with gleaming coats as white as snow and as soft as the finest down. She lived in the countryside, surrounded by fields. What an idyllic and peaceful setting it was—until I got inside the house. Maltese are known to have particularly fine voices, and all five of her dogs barked continually throughout the day. One of the first questions I ask any owner is how much exercise their dogs receive. My client replied that she didn't walk her dogs because they were show dogs and she didn't want their coats to split or become matted. I'm not often rendered speechless, but in this instance I could do nothing but stand and stare at her. How could an experienced dog owner not understand that her dogs were barking because they were bored and stressed from lack of physical exercise and mental stimulation? Despite my advice to meet her dogs' needs, the woman continued to keep them in pent-up torment, all because she enjoyed winning dog shows. I was appalled.

Enriching your dog's life doesn't need to take up a lot of time. It just means a different approach: a new awareness of your dog's needs and a few small life changes. Walking is good for people too, so sharing the responsibility with the whole family ensures that your dog receives the attention and time he deserves and everyone stays fit. A tired dog is a happy dog!

QUICK TIPS TO PREVENT BOREDOM

Here are some great ways to keep your dog physically and mentally enriched:

- Stimulate your dog's senses by allowing him to experience
  different environments each day. Introduce new smells,
  sights, sounds, tastes, and textures in your home, around the
  neighborhood, or at your local park.

- If your dog spends long hours at home by himself during the
  day, consider hiring a dog walker or take your dog to a reputable doggy day care. Leaving your dog in the yard all day
  without taking him for a walk is as bad as leaving him in the
  house—the "backyard barker" is an all too familiar sound.

- If your dog loves the car, take him for a ride. This provides
  great visual stimulation and that "wind in the face" thrill.

- Play games with your dog, such as hide-and-seek, fetch, foot-
  ball, Frisbee, and tug-of-war. Hide treats around the house
  and activate your dog's "seeker system" by sending him on
  a treasure hunt. Vary your dog's toys by rotating them each
  day; buy toys that challenge his brain, such as a durable rubber toy, treat ball, or puzzle.

- Teach your dog new action cues, such as "sit," "lie down,"
  "touch," "go to bed," "wait," and "come," to provide valuable
  mental stimulation. There are many examples of great action
  cues you can teach throughout this book.

- Find an agility class in your area and get together with other
  owners and their dogs. Agility is a sport where dogs learn to
  go over a number of obstacles in varying sequences. It is the
  perfect sport to challenge your dog mentally and physically
  while encouraging both of you to work as a team. Not only
  is it beautiful to watch, but mastering new moves provides a

much-needed confidence boost, especially for dogs that have insecurity or anxiety issues.

- Organize a regular dog-walking group or set up canine play dates. Playing helps a dog rehearse his social skills and keeps him active.

- Sports such as Canine Freestyle and Rally Obedience teach your dog to be in tune with your every movement while developing great communication skills and creating a stronger bond between you.

- Cater to your dog's needs by allowing his breed or mix of breeds to dictate what he may enjoy doing. If your dog is predisposed to tracking, hunting, luring, or herding, there are many organizations you can join throughout the country that practice these specific sports in controlled environments.

- If your dog likes to be touched, give him a massage. This is a good way to relax and increases the bond between you.

- Therapy work can be great for the confident, social dog. These dogs love visiting the elderly and people in hospitals or schools because they thrive on human attention.

- Minimize destruction by managing your dog's environment, and set him up for success by providing him with a safe area where he can go when unsupervised.

The Ultimate Separation Distress and Anxiety Treatment Plan

As I've discussed, dogs that suffer from separation issues can create anything from minor to major destruction when left alone. This destruction is focused not only on points of entry, but also in places and with objects that are more intimately associated with an owner, such as shoes, beds, or sofas. Chewing eases frustration and promotes a feeling of calm for a dog—just as some humans relieve tension by biting their nails. Some dogs will chew on themselves or household objects; others may develop displacement/obsessive type behaviors such as repeated pacing, spinning, or licking.

Bob, a cute little Boston Terrier, belonged to Shirley, a young lawyer who spent many hours working away from home. The Boston Terrier is known to be a lively breed; Bob was a firework waiting to explode. Shirley told me how much he liked to suck on blankets and bath towels, nibbling off the labels perfectly without harming the rest of the material. Strangely, Shirley kept Bob's detached labels in a bag as souvenirs of his delicate work. There were hundreds of them!

The real problem arose, however, whenever Shirley left for work in the morning. As soon as she started putting on her make-up, Bob would pace up and down the apartment, salivating profusely. Putting on make-up was the beginning of Shirley's "departure ritual" and the first in a long line of triggers that told Bob she was leaving him. By the time Shirley left the apartment, Bob was in a state of panic. Neighbors reported that he barked for half an hour after Shirley had left and in spurts throughout the day. By the time Shirley came back nine hours later, Bob was beside himself with excitement, jumping and nibbling at her as she struggled to get through the door. By then the apartment was in a state of utter disarray. Pillows and sofas had been chewed, walls gnawed, and the front door scratched. Urine and feces were everywhere. Shirley and Bob needed help.

The choice of a management protocol for the treatment of separation distress and anxiety depends on the severity of the disorder, which must be tackled on many levels. First and foremost, anxious dogs require appropriate daily exercise to lessen their anxiety and increase their ability to cope, being particularly effective if done just before an owner's departure. Shirley needed to get up a little earlier in the mornings and give Bob good aerobic exercise rather than the usual ten-minute pee-and-poop walk. This daily exercise was complemented with an active training program that allowed Bob to learn new action cues centered on impulse control and problem solving, designed to stimulate the learning part of his brain and ease his frustration.

Even though Shirley was flattered that Bob followed her everywhere and adored the ground she walked on, indulging this habit did not help him, so she focused on developing a more balanced, less dependent relationship while she was at home. If she needed to use the bathroom, she was to go in and close the door, leaving Bob outside. At times she would take herself off to her bedroom and shut the door so that Bob was left in the living room, sometimes with a toy to work on. This separation in the home was new to him and took some getting used to, but after a few days, he became less bothered when he was left in a room by himself.

It was much easier for Bob to cope with Shirley's departure if she didn't make a fuss over him when she was leaving. The same was true when she returned, so we worked on making Shirley's entrances and exits no big deal. She was to say a soft "good-bye" when she left and a quiet "hello" when she returned and then go about her business until Bob was calm so that they could relax together. Bob was also very sensitive to changes in his environment, so the transition from the energy when Shirley was present to the silence in the home when she left was profound. I asked her to start leaving lights on and playing music in the apartment when she was away.

DESENSITIZATION TO DEPARTURE TRIGGERS

Desensitizing dogs to departure triggers is an important part of any good behavior modification plan, as some dogs become anxious as soon as they see their owners picking up keys and putting on coats. Masking these triggers by hiding coats, putting keys in a different place, and using a different handbag can help, but dogs quickly become wise to our human tricks, and an owner's departure energy is difficult to hide. However, putting on a coat and exiting the home followed immediately by a return allows a dog to see the trigger in a different light. The dog learns that the act of putting on a coat does not necessarily signal an owner is going to leave for a long period of time. Constant repetition over a number of days helps desensitize the dog until departures no longer trigger a response. Time spent away is gradually increased until the dog is confident that the owner will always return.

Shirley started by putting on her coat, walking out the door for a few seconds, returning, removing her coat, and sitting down. She repeated this many times, gradually getting to one minute and then building up to five minutes by the end of our session. By the twentieth departure, Bob began to lose interest in what Shirley was doing. The first thirty minutes after an owner's departure can be the worst for a dog that suffers from separation problems, so building up the time slowly was critical, and Bob's response was exactly what we wanted to see. Shirley and I were exhausted, but Bob was quiet and had taken himself off to his bed. Breakthrough!

SOUND THERAPY

Sound therapy is a form of *sensory education* that is a new and exciting addition to any behavior modification protocol dealing with anxiety or stress issues in dogs. I have long used music to aid the relaxation process, and I had always wanted to find a way of combining music with certain behavior modification techniques to create an even more powerful and effective way to ease anxieties and phobias in dogs. I have seen the profound effect that the specially designed psychoacoustic music of Through a Dog's Ear has on calming dogs in homes and shelters around the world, but I wanted to go a step further by combining this music with a behavior modification plan to help calm a dog's nervous system. So I teamed up with the founders of Through a Dog's Ear: concert pianist Lisa Spector and Joshua Leeds, a noted sound researcher who has studied the effect of music and sound on the human and canine nervous system. Leeds explains that auditory cognition in humans is complex but, "when exposed to music, the human brain methodically analyzes every interval, rhythmic nuance, instrumental density, and melodic turn." His innovative research found that many of the same auditory cues also affect canines. For many years, Leeds and Spector tested their groundbreaking music on dogs in all kind of situations and in many different environments, discovering that dogs showed a preference for slow, simple classical music played on a solo piano at a low frequency.[1]

To begin the process of habituating Bob to the music, I advised that Shirley find a time when she and Bob could either relax together or engage in a low-energy activity that he enjoyed while playing the *Calming* CD from the Canine Noise Phobia Series (which I developed in partnership with Through a Dog's Ear; see Resources). Pairing the music with activities that Bob enjoyed helped him relax and built up a positive association with the music being played. This association was "charged" over a period of days by repeating the music at intervals during periods of calm. Once a positive association with the music had been made and Shirley could be away from home for five minutes without Bob panicking, she then turned on the music as soon as she walked back into the apartment. This protocol was designed so that Bob would not only associate the music with good things but also recognize that the music signaled her return as well. Repeating this process ensured that he now recognized her "arrival" music, which could then be played *before* she was about to leave and during the first forty-five minutes after she left. So that the music never became a precursor cue to Shirley's leaving, she also continued to play it at intervals when she was at home.

THE HEALING POWER OF TOYS AND FOOD

Leaving a dog with appropriate activity toys on which to chew is a crucial element of managing separation distress. Some dogs are too anxious to eat or play with a toy when their owner is absent, so it's important to introduce the dog's favorite toys and/or chews while the owner is present, building up a positive feeling around that particular toy. This toy is then given to the dog a few minutes before the owner departs, in the hope that the dog will be more focused on the toy than on the owner's departure. Interactive toys such as stuffed rubber bones or treat balls can also help refocus the mind, encouraging the dog to release anxious energy on an appropriate item rather than the sofa. Initially, Bob couldn't eat or play with anything when Shirley was away, but by providing a positive association with the toys while she was present, Shirley helped him gradually enjoy them while she was gone.

Despite good progress from the institution of these management protocols, Shirley's schedule of nine hours a day, five days a week was still a problem. It was a long time to leave Bob by himself. Dogs don't do well in social isolation, so we had to do something to break up the monotony of his day. Luckily Shirley was in a position to invest in a dog walker three times a week, and twice a week Bob went to doggy day care, which he loved. Bob's behavior improved immeasurably, and Shirley could finally feel confident that she was coming home to a happier dog—and an intact apartment.

WHAT'S ON TV?

A recent study revealed that about one-fifth of all American pet owners leave their TV or radio on for their pets.[2] The problem is that the television channels our pets end up watching or listening to too often do more harm than good because constant talk becomes an overpowering irritant or the programming contains loud music or sounds interspersed with even louder commercials, meaning the dog never receives an auditory break.

Luckily, production companies are aware of this issue and have begun offering video products and actual TV channels like DogTV, which are specifically designed to be watched by canines. The best of these offerings are steadfastly committed to providing both an aural and visual environment that is tailored specifically to the needs of today's domesticated dog. The colors and frequencies of the visual and audio content on these channels are specially designed to resonate positively with our canine companions (see Canine Senses: Sight in chapter 4). Another aspect of TV for dogs that breaks new ground is that it doesn't simply attempt to calm a dog that may otherwise suffer from anxiety. Those of us in the field of animal behavior who are involved with DogTV have helped make sure that the channel's 24/7 content follows certain timing rhythms.

If you invest in one of these channels for your dog, be aware that rather than simply playing calming music and showing pictures of lulling ocean surf, the content also slowly introduces and alternates between scenes that are more stimulating from a dog's point of view. This will ensure that throughout the lonely hours a dog is home with this channel on in the background, there are periods of subtly increased motion and tempo. As a result, the dog will be periodically and almost imperceptibly stimulated, helping to minimize the boredom that can often result in destructive behavior. This type of content is also interspersed with periods of "exposure" in which dogs might hear, for example, the distant sound of a vacuum cleaner played at very low levels, providing gradually increasing sound effects that effectively desensitize dogs to everyday domestic environmental sounds and help prevent noise sensitivities and phobias from ever occurring.

Channels like DogTV are not designed to become "must see TV" for our dogs, and it's perfectly okay for dogs not to want to become couch "pet-atoes" once they're switched on. To the contrary, the real value in TV for dogs can be found in those long hours when we're not around and our dogs are otherwise either completely unstimulated or suffering from separation distress.

Appropriate video content for canines is just one of many valuable tools available to help ease our dogs' loneliness and provide comfort during separation. I advise all pet parents to make time to watch the content with their dog for short periods over a couple of days or have the channel on in the background when home. This ensures that every dog's reaction to the content can be monitored—because if a dog barks at or rushes the television, DogTV is not right for him. Introducing the channel when the owner is present will help provide a positive association between the content and the comfort of the owner's presence, making it easier for the dog to cope when his owners leave.

COMPLEMENTARY THERAPIES

There are many other complementary therapies that can be used with behavior modification. Undetectable by humans, Dog Appeasing Pheromone is a synthetically produced product that mimics the pheromones of a lactating female and is said to produce a feeling of well-being and reassurance for dogs, thereby reducing anxiety. It's available in spray form and as a plug-in or can be contained in a collar worn around a dog's neck. Lavender essence remedies can also help lessen anxiety, as can massage and other similar therapies such as Reiki. I am generally a skeptic, but I once witnessed a Reiki master put a rambunctious Standard Schnauzer into a trance just by holding his hands an inch away from the dog's body. The dog was in such a state of relaxation after ten minutes of "hand hovering" that he soon fell asleep. I saw the same thing watching a Basset Hound go through acupuncture. Anxious dogs might also feel calmer when wearing a tightly wrapped coat, just as a baby calms when it's swaddled. I encourage my clients to try natural remedies like these to relieve their dog's stress, unless the anxiety is so pronounced that the dog is unable to focus or learn anything. In such cases a veterinarian or veterinary behaviorist can prescribe medication that will help the dog get to a calmer state where learning can occur.

MEDICATION

Dogs that are too stressed to respond to behavior modification may need extra help to take the edge off their stress. Using mood stabilizing medication with a behavior modification plan can sometimes make all the difference in bringing a dog to the point where he is able to learn. Dr. Dodman points out that medication can be used with or without behavior modification, and even though this may encourage some people to rely on medication alone, he makes the fair point that in reality some people don't have the time or ability to follow what can be a time-consuming teaching plan.[3] Most of these mood-enhancing modern drugs do not cause sedation, nor do they negatively affect a dog's memory or ability to learn. A dog on these medications will in fact find learning easier as the anxiety lessens. Prozac, a selective serotonin reuptake inhibitor (SSRI) that blocks the reuptake of serotonin in the brain, has been found to be a highly effective treatment for separation anxiety. Although some behavioral scientists might argue that too much emphasis is being put on the relationship between serotonin and mood, I have seen many anxious dogs improve dramatically when prescribed drugs like Prozac (a brand name for fluoxetine). As with any behavioral issue, however, it is vitally important that you take your dog for a full medical checkup to rule out any medical causes and to talk to your veterinarian about medications that may improve your dog's behavior.

Whether you use complementary therapies or medication, always remember that one tool alone is usually not enough to overcome an issue as significant as separation distress. I believe these therapies should always be combined with a behavior modification protocol, and more serious cases usually require the assistance of a qualified positive reinforcement–based dog trainer.

Tips to Ease Separation Distress and Anxiety

- Start by taking your dog to the veterinarian to rule out any medical cause for anxiety.
- Increase your dog's daily activity; schedule exercise for a good hour before you are due to leave home.
- Go back to teaching 101! Teach activity cues that focus on impulse control and problem solving.
- Teach independence while you are home by routinely separating yourself from your dog, especially when you go to the bathroom, take a shower, or read a book.
- Make it easier for your dog to cope with your absence by building up a positive association with music from the Canine Noise Phobia Series *Calming* CD.
- Desensitize your dog to departure triggers. Constant repetitions of departures and immediate returns can aid desensitization.

- Vary your departure cues.
- Pair your departure with something pleasant by leaving your dog with high-value chew toys.
- Even out emotional highs and lows by not giving your dog too much attention when you leave or return home.
- Build up the time you are away from the home in small increments. Your dog will dictate the pace, but take care not to go too far, too fast.
- If you work during the day, consider taking your dog to doggy day care or hiring a dog walker.
- If you have a channel like DogTV in your area, subscribe!
- Use a video camera to record your dog's progress.
- If your dog is too stressed to learn, consult with your veterinarian about using medication to complement a behavioral modification plan.

In conclusion, dogs that find it hard to be alone need to be handled sensitively, as panic upon separation is a terrible fear to experience—particularly on a daily basis. Because there is no way to tell your dog that your absence is only temporary, success depends on your being present during the training process or having your dog with others at all times when you cannot be there. The more your dog experiences anxiety, the harder it will be to change his mind-set, but if his anxiety levels are kept low throughout because you have made arrangements never to leave him by himself during the modification process, a successful outcome is much more likely.

8

STRESS, ANXIETY, AND FEAR

From Thunderstorm Phobia to Compulsive Behavior

It is now generally accepted, based on decades of research, that dogs not only experience emotions but also suffer from some of the same emotional problems that people do, such as anxiety, depression, anger, fear, compulsive disorders, and phobias. Unfortunately, I see many dogs with emotional issues like these that make it hard for them to cope with everyday life. Like people, some dogs are more sensitive than others to the mental and physical manifestations of stress, so what may cause sickness in one dog may have little effect on another even when both are exposed to the same stressors. Although occasional mild stress can actually be healthy, providing beneficial physical and mental stimulation, research has shown that there is a link between chronic stress and illnesses such as heart disease and gastrointestinal disorders. Whether or not these diseases are actually caused by stress is still unknown, but they are exacerbated by a stressful lifestyle, making understanding and management of these disorders vital for a longer, healthier life.

Pet dogs are impressively adaptive. The ability to cope with new environments and situations is a product of their domestication, and most dogs do extremely well adapting to the pressures of domestic life. There are some, however, that find it hard to adjust and consequently live in a constant state of stress, making life difficult for themselves and for their owners.

Understanding how stress affects our canine companions is easier once you realize that dogs and humans have very similar physiological responses to stress. During a stressful episode (let's say you and your dog are being chased), both the human and the canine body experience adaptive changes. For human or dog to survive, energy must immediately be diverted to certain muscles in preparation for fight or flight. Glucose, fats, and proteins pour out of the liver, fat cells, and unused muscles and are sent to the muscles needing the most energy. Heart rate and blood pressure are elevated in order to distribute the energy as quickly as possible, while breathing becomes more rapid to meet the demand for more oxygen. Digestion is suppressed, the immune system is inhibited, and senses are sharpened. This all happens within a matter of seconds and allows the body to operate at its optimum level to ensure survival.

Under normal conditions it usually takes about two days for the stress hormone cortisol to leave a dog's body after a traumatic episode. Humans tend to have a harder time returning to "normal" because of their ability to dwell on, anticipate, or expect future problems, but dogs that are sensitive to the triggers that predict certain outcomes or that are frequently exposed to something they fear can also find it hard to de-stress. Good health depends on the body's ability to return to its normal state after the stressful event, but if the body continues to work at its optimum level and is unable to return to normal, it's only a matter of time before the immune system is impaired, opening the door to adaptive illnesses such as kidney disease, diabetes, and cancer.

Stressed and fearful dogs are often highly reactive and unable to settle, jumping at the slightest sound or movement. This is due to an overproduction of hormones like cortisol and adrenaline. These hormones foster a constant state of arousal in the brain as if the dog anticipates a life-threatening event at every turn. This impedes the learning brain from rationally deciding what is and is not threatening. A lack of serotonin and dopamine, the two neurotransmitters in the brain that help modulate responses and emotional activity, mixed with a high level of stress hormones makes it very hard for a dog to listen and focus on anything for more than a few seconds.

Sunny was a fearful three-year-old Terrier mix who reacted to every small sound and visual stimulus in her environment, and there was nothing her owner could do to calm her down. Sunny was in a constant state of alert inside and outside the home, scanning her surroundings as if she anticipated a threat to come at her from all sides. This made it very hard for her to cope with any kind of social situation or change in environment. Her brain continually operated in panic mode, and her attention shifted so rapidly from one thing to another that she barely had time to breathe. The poor dog was completely overwhelmed.

The stress and fear that dogs like Sunny experience are manifested in physiological symptoms such as dilated pupils, sweaty paws, shaking, and salivating. Other expressions come in the form of self-calming techniques (such as yawning and lip licking) or intense displacement behavior (such as sniffing, excessive grooming, spinning, or self-mutilation). These dogs may urinate or defecate more frequently and also suffer from digestive upset such as diarrhea. Some dogs may display symptoms that look very much like human depression, including the inability to sleep, low energy, lack of appetite, and a limited desire for human or dog interaction. Learned helplessness, wherein the dog shuts down, is often misunderstood as a dog becoming "calm submissive." It is yet another symptom of stress that can occur if a dog is severely punished or suffers abuse. Aggressive behaviors such as growling, snapping, and biting are common symptoms of stress.

We now know that dogs also suffer from something very similar to the human form of post-traumatic stress disorder (PTSD). Dr. Frank McMillan of Best Friends Animal Sanctuary states that a single or chronic exposure to a stressful or traumatic event may alter synaptic nerves, resulting in chemical changes that increase anxiety-related behaviors such as hyperreactivity, flashbacks, avoidance, mood swings, irritability, "snapping" (not just a biting action, but the dog's complete loss of control), insomnia, shut down, and depression.[1] Humans are able to assess, talk about, and analyze a traumatic event; dogs, however, cannot rationalize and tell themselves there is nothing to be scared of. Instinct tells them to fear because this keeps them safe.

Research has shown that the better humans and animals can predict and control outcomes in certain situations, the better their ability to cope.[2] When a dog's fear is so intense that it interferes with normal life, his natural ability to acquire knowledge is inhibited and his quality of life is negatively affected.[3]

So what can you do to minimize stress for your dogs, particularly if you have a super-anxious dog like Sunny? First, it's important to realize that dogs do not have the ability or intellectual desire to "change" themselves, so human intervention is required to help them adapt by using techniques that promote emotional change. Helping your dog learn via gradual desensitization, counterconditioning techniques, management of her exposure to stressors, and confidence-building exercises can be of great help.

Minimizing potential stressors at home and watching how you manage your own stress is important, as dogs are very good at picking up on a person's emotional state.

Controlled exercise is also a great way to alleviate stress and fear both for dogs and people, as exercise improves cognitive function, encourages confidence, stabilizes mood, and reduces reactivity while improving the relationship between dog and owner. Developing coping strategies—such as playing problem-solving games and using toys—can help activate a dog's thinking brain in stressful situations, which in turn deactivates the emotional brain and allows the dog to concentrate on something more positive than the negative emotion. (For example, I'm writing this on a plane that is flying close to a thunderstorm. The plane is being tossed around like a tin can, but concentrating on writing this chapter is preventing me from having the complete emotional meltdown that I might otherwise be having if I were sitting on the plane with nothing else to do but worry.)

Thunderstorm Phobia

Working with dogs that have a fear or phobia can be complex, because even though some common fears can be successfully managed, others are so deeply ingrained that they are difficult to change. Thunderstorm phobia is relatively common for dogs, particularly for those that live in areas where stormy weather is commonplace. Recent reports have shown that 93 percent of dogs with noise phobias fear thunder and other loud noises, including fireworks.[4] Whether fear of thunderstorms is caused by a single traumatic experience or prolonged exposure, the result is often highly distressing for dogs and owners. Without extensive behavioral therapy and management strategies, phobias become deeply ingrained and even harder to overcome.

I live in the southeastern United States where thunderstorms are a common occurrence, particularly in the spring and hot summer months. The intensity and frequency of these thunderstorms can be frightening for anyone, but some dogs are so traumatized that they are unable to function normally for hours before and during a thunderstorm. Many thunderstorm-phobic dogs adopt self-management strategies to cope, attempting to escape from the home, digging into carpets, seeking out dark denlike spaces in which to hide, pacing, or crawling behind a bathroom sink or toilet.

What makes behavioral modification in these cases so difficult is that thunderstorms are not easy to predict or control. A dog usually knows when a storm is coming long before a human does and becomes increasingly panicked as it approaches.

It's possible to condition a dog to feel differently about storm noise by gradually exposing the dog to audio recordings of storm sounds at low volume levels and, if she appears relaxed, playing her favorite game or feeding her her favorite food. Allowing a dog to play and relax in the presence of the soft noise for short periods of time throughout the day ensures that she does not become bored with the training. Introducing the audio at a low level and gradually turning up the volume allows the dog to habituate to the noise without a fear response.

I have taken this gradual adaptation process a step further by pairing clinically demonstrated psycho-acoustic calming music (the same kind of music I use for dogs that suffer with separation anxiety) with gradually increasing levels of thunderstorm sound effects. This ground-breaking complement to sensory education from my Canine Noise Phobia Series helps dogs acclimate to thunderstorm sounds in a controlled environment. The recording is uniquely constructed to enable dogs to "tune out" the sounds of a thunderstorm. In addition to treating already present thunderstorm phobias, this tool can be used to prevent thunderstorm noise phobia and other noise sensitivities from ever developing (see Resources).

The goal of this therapy is to change how a dog feels by altering the way she hears the sound. My noise desensitization CDs encourage nervous dogs to *passively hear* the noise rather than *actively listen* to it. As you read this chapter, you may not be aware of other noises around you, even though you are indeed passively hearing them. Stop reading (for just a moment) and concentrate on the sounds in your environment. Even though they've been there all the time, you haven't registered them until now because you haven't been *actively listening* to them. Start reading again, and after a while your brain will shut out the sounds around you even though those sounds are still present. You may even become aware of them again, but they probably won't bother you if you're truly engaged in what you're reading. For a dog, the end result of this noise desensitization process is that, even though she hears a thunderstorm, the sound no longer overwhelms or scares her.

Gradually exposing a dog to flashes of light (by using the flash of a camera, but not in the dog's face) that grow in intensity and using fans to simulate increasing wind are complementary parts of this therapy, but these can sometimes be harder to implement. Some dogs respond well to all of these tools during teaching sessions but may still become panicked when a real storm rolls in. It's therefore important to tackle this phobia in other ways by using effective management strategies and masking any visual stimuli that elicit a fear response during a storm.

Dogs can be very sensitive to changes in barometric pressure that occur before a storm, but there is also a hypothesis that some dogs—especially long-coated breeds—become statically charged during a thunderstorm, receiving electric shocks from static in the air unless they "ground" themselves. It's believed that dogs do this by retreating to a bathroom and hiding behind a sink or toilet, staying close to pipes that provide electrical grounding. If the hypothesis is true, it would certainly explain why so many dogs end up cowering in a bathroom. To reduce static build-up, some owners wipe their dogs down with antistatic laundry strips and spray antistatic spray on their dogs' paws, but care should be taken to avoid using products that contain harmful chemicals that dogs could lick off .[5]

The most important thing you can do for your thunderstorm-phobic dog is to provide her with a "bolt hole"—a place she can escape to in the event of a storm. Providing access to this safe place is essential at all times, particularly if you are absent. This could be a closet, bathroom, or basement (the best places usually have no windows), but with plenty of artificial light to mask flashes of lightning. If static electricity is a problem, rubber matting or tile is a good antistatic material to use for flooring. Calming music should be played close to the safe haven to mask the sounds of thunder. If you are present during the storm, spend time with your dog in the safe haven or give her attention if she comes to seek comfort. Far from reinforcing fearful behavior, your presence will help your dog cope—as long as you remain calm.

Some phobic dogs benefit from chewing on a food-stuffed toy or calming therapies such as TTouch, anxiety wraps, pheromone collars, and lavender essence; others do much better on anti-anxiety medication that can be given just before a thunderstorm or by daily dosage, especially during storm season. It is vital that behavioral therapy and management are always implemented in tandem with any medication, to give the dog the best possible chance of rehabilitation. Thunderstorm phobia is a difficult condition to treat, but trying a variety of therapies and techniques can help dogs cope when the big clouds roll in.

Obsessive Compulsive Disorders

A friend of mine exercised his Labrador puppy in the backyard each night by encouraging his dog to chase a beam of light from a laser that he shone on the ground. He now wonders why his adult dog is unable to focus on anything except lights and reflections either inside or outside the home. This dog's compulsive light chasing looks very like the human form of obsessive-compulsive disorder (OCD), a potentially disabling psychiatric condition in which obsessive thoughts and compulsive actions such as hand washing, cleaning, hair plucking, or hoarding take over a person's life.[6] Scientists and behavior professionals still debate whether we should call the canine form of compulsive disorder "obsessive," because we don't know what dogs are thinking, so the condition in some circles is referred to as *canine compulsive disorder* (CCD). However, I see so many cases where dogs seem obsessively compelled to indulge in repetitive behaviors that I'm absolutely convinced what I'm seeing is an obsessive disorder as well as a compulsion.

Canine OCD is exacerbated by anxiety, frustration, and stress, but there is a genetic component as well, as many breeds suffer from specific types of repetitive behavior. Spinning and tail chasing are prevalent in Bull Terriers and German Shepherds; Dobermans are more prone to blanket- or flank-sucking. Canine OCD can develop in dogs that lead sensory-deprived lives when their basic or breed-specific needs are not met. These dogs find other ways to cope with this deprivation by indulging in repetitive actions—such as pacing, spinning, and licking—that serve no meaningful function whatsoever except as an outlet for their pent-up stress and frustration. The more these dogs indulge in repetitive behaviors, the more ingrained these behaviors become, until they simply cannot stop. Repetitive or displacement actions are self-soothing at first and act as a release valve for extra energy, but when they take over a dog's life, behaviors that previously soothed the dog now actually increase the distress. Humans contribute to and exacerbate canine OCD by confining their dogs for long hours in crates or small kennel runs, failing to provide outlets for their dog's energy, or treating their dogs harshly. Canine OCD has also been linked to seizure disorders and abnormal brain function, which is why deeply ingrained compulsions usually require medical intervention with anticonvulsant or antiobsessional medication. This condition can manifest itself in many different ways, each requiring careful consideration when determining how best to try to manage them.

SPINNING AND TAIL CHASING

Rocky the Wheaten Terrier bounced off the walls and spun in place whenever a guest or family member came through the front door. Rocky had a history of biting strangers, so his family kept him separated from their guests, but this confinement caused such frustration that he exploded whenever the doorbell rang, twirling and ricocheting off the walls in the hallway.

Displacement behaviors such as spinning and licking normally occur as an occasional response to a stressful episode. These behaviors become obsessive, however, when they occur in other environments and situations without a particular event that triggers the behavior. By the time I arrived to help Rocky, his spinning was occurring in other locations around the home, without the trigger of the doorbell, and couldn't be stopped unless his family physically interrupted him.

The great sadness in this case was that it could have been easily solved if the family had taken more responsibility for Rocky and actually walked him. They had six capable people living in the home who could have shared the responsibility, but they fought constantly about who was going to do it. Considering some of the things I've seen during my career, I shouldn't be surprised by the way people behave anymore, but this family was particularly shameful. They spent more time arguing with each other than focusing on helping their dog get better. Dr. Dodman, an expert in canine OCD, even came to provide additional assistance, but the family refused to follow through with the generous support that was offered.

When I took Rocky and his family to a large off-leash space to see how he behaved, he became a different dog. The pure joy I saw on his face as he ran around the field was a testament to how much he enjoyed and needed this daily outlet. As he raced around the open fields, the family was delighted to see their usually anxious dog so happy, but I had little confidence that they would continue to exercise him in this way after I had gone. Even though Rocky showed great improvement during my time with him, repeated attempts to maintain contact with the family and monitor his progress failed, and a year later I heard that he had been rehomed. I hope he is having a better life with people who actually care about his well-being.

When I met Lottie she, too, spun around in circles, but she had a valid reason: she was hell-bent on trying to catch her tail. It infuriated her that the furry little nub above her backside was just out of her reach, but that didn't stop her from trying. Lottie had been rescued from a backyard breeder who kept all his puppies and dogs in tiny crates, and I believe her tail chasing had entertained and soothed her during her confinement. Even with a new home, a loving family, and more space around her, the behavior was so deeply ingrained that she continued to chase her tail whenever she got the chance.

Dogs that chase their tails tend to have high prey drive, and Lottie was no exception. Each time she spun, her tail moved away from her like prey trying to escape.

Because of Lottie's high drive, she had a tendency to run away on walks, and the family didn't feel confident walking her off the leash. I gave them a long line and an extendable leash so that she would safely get the exercise she needed while building up a reliable recall. Extendable leashes should only be used in open areas, and care should be taken to ensure that dogs don't hurt themselves. Used correctly, however, this leash was a godsend that allowed the family to take Lottie into the woods and give her stimulating outside experiences. I also found a fenced-in field that they could use where Lottie could run with abandon and indulge her love of chasing prey by going after the balls and squeaky toys the family threw for her.

Increased exercise and mental stimulation helped Lottie calm down when she was at home, and her spinning decreased indoors. The backyard still seemed to trigger the behavior, however, so we limited access and only allowed Lottie out when she was actively playing with her family. I also purchased long agility tunnels and arranged them in straight lines around the yard to encourage her to go forward rather than round and round in circles!

AIR SNAPPING

Interestingly, some dogs appear to watch and bite at imaginary flies in front of their face—a behavior particularly prevalent among some breeds, including German Shepherds and Cavalier King Charles Spaniels. There are a number of suspected causes for this behavior, including partial epileptic seizures, hallucinations, and, in Cavaliers, a devastating disease called *syringomyelia*. When the cerebrospinal fluid is prevented from circulating normally between the brain and spinal cord due to a narrowing or blockage of the flow, this forces the fluid into the spinal cord at a higher than normal rate, causing the spinal cord to expand or pull apart, creating a cavity and squeezing fluid from blood vessels and other tissues into the cavity.[7] This causes migraine-like headaches and pain around the neck and shoulders that the dog tries to ease by snapping or scratching at its neck. A study in Sweden by Dr. Jens Haggstrom demonstrated that fly snapping could also be linked to a condition known as *idiopathic asymptomatic thrombocytopenia*, which causes an abnormally low level of blood platelets, affecting the circulation of blood in the brain.[8] Dogs that exhibit this behavior require a full medical examination to rule out the possibility of a serious medical condition or seizure activity, but if a clean bill of health is given, the behavior could be a compulsion, depending on the context in which it happens. As with all compulsive behaviors, a full behavioral history and evaluation should be taken and the appropriate therapies prescribed, with medication if needed.

FLANK AND BLANKET SUCKING

Before Sadie came into our home at the age of five, she had lived a pretty boring life. She was hugely overweight but nevertheless would lunge at other dogs when they passed by. She had spent the first five years of her life with an elderly woman who gave her plenty of love but couldn't walk her, and as a result Sadie spent her days licking her paws and chewing on her flank. I wasn't so concerned about the licking, because I knew she suffered from allergies that made her paws itch, but the flank sucking was something of a mystery. At first I thought she might be targeting her flank to relieve referred pain from somewhere else in her body, but after further study it became evident that it was a habit that gave her comfort. It almost looked like she was nursing on herself, and indeed dogs that indulge in this behavior do so to soothe themselves, rather like a baby sucking on a pacifier. Puppies gain food and comfort from their mother when nursing, and sometimes after weaning, this need for comfort is transferred to something different such as a blanket, human skin, or the dog's own body.

As soon as Sadie came to us, her life was enriched by exercise, activities, and positive attention. This redirected her licking and flank sucking almost overnight, but there were still times when she reverted to her old habits. During quiet times of the day, I fastened a surgery cone around her neck, a temporary solution that inhibited her ability to practice the behavior while I investigated other causes and solutions. I wouldn't recommend using a cone full time, as most dogs despise them, but Sadie's flank had been raw and red from her chewing, and the wound needed to heal. After a thorough medical check-up I discovered she was hypothyroid (thyroid issues have been shown to exacerbate flank-sucking behavior[9]); with the medication she was prescribed to stabilize her hormone levels, increased attention, and more exercise, her flank sucking eventually became a thing of the past.

LIGHT AND SHADOW CHASING

Max was a magnificent Gordon Setter who had an obsession for chasing reflections and shadows inside and outside the home. This made working with him very difficult, because whenever he saw a flicker of light he stopped whatever he was doing, fixated on it as if in a trance, and then licked where the shadow or reflection had been. Teaching outside on a sunny day was impossible, and the only way I could snap him out of his fixation was to put on his leash and physically walk him away.

Max's intense fixation and licking had to be redirected onto something more positive. His exercise needs were being met, but his home environment had to be managed. It was very hard for his family to cook anything in the kitchen, for example, because Max tried to chase the reflections made by the metal pans used for cooking. For his own and his family's safety, he was kept out of the kitchen whenever meals were being prepared. As I do with all the compulsive dogs I meet, I enriched his environment in other ways by giving him interactive toys and feeding him his meals in nonreflective treat balls rather than from his bowl. Max had great hunting, seeking, and problem-solving skills, so I was pleased to see that he now spent more time working with the toys and puzzles I gave him than staring at reflections.

I eventually learned that Max had started life as a mascot for an army regiment in Scotland. His home was the regiment's ballroom, which was lined from floor to ceiling with mirrors. When the sun shone, light reflected from all sides, which meant he must have spent many hours entertaining himself by chasing the reflections made by the mirrors. In Max's case it seemed that situational reinforcement had helped encourage a light-chasing habit that had quickly gotten out of control.

LICKING

I don't see many cases in which both dog and owner demonstrate repetitive, compulsive behavior, but Zulu, a Boxer, and his owner, Mark, were an exception. Zulu had recently moved with his family from a large home in South Africa to a tiny condo near Heathrow, London, so the dog had gone from a huge backyard to one that he could barely run in. Rather than running, as he had used to do, Zulu spent all his pent-up energy jumping up onto the eight-foot-high fence his owners had built around the small yard. He never made it to the top, but his jumping made the family nervous. Zulu's frustration also manifested itself in his constant licking of household objects and people, including sofas, chairs, curtains, clothes, carpets, and Mark's bald head, a behavior that Mark actively encouraged. Interestingly, Mark also suffered from a compulsive disorder. He obsessed about his furniture getting scratched and spent a good deal of his free time inspecting his home; even a tiny scratch meant the furniture had to be replaced. His compulsion had become worse after the transfer because he missed his former home so much. As I walked around the house, making sure I didn't touch anything, it was obvious to me that both dog and owner had been stressed out by the move.

Some dogs are prone to compulsive self-grooming on a particular area of the body, causing wounds to form and making them hard to heal. This is called *acral lick dermatitis* (ALD) or *lick granuloma*, but licking can also occur on other areas, objects, or materials as a displacement behavior for a dog's boredom or anxiety, resulting in an obsessive behavior that is hard to change. It was evident that Zulu's dramatic change of environment had made the licking worse, and of course, as in so many cases I see, he needed more exercise. I provided Zulu with an assortment of activity toys and puzzles that were rotated each day and given at certain times when his licking was more likely to occur. Because he loved to jump, he started agility classes at the local training club. In addition to increased exercise, I encouraged the family to play with him as much as they could in their tiny backyard and implement a teaching program to engage his brain and redirect the licking onto something more appropriate. Mark admitted that the hardest behavior to change was his own, as he loved the feeling of Zulu licking his bald head!

Zulu's compulsion resolved with behavioral therapy, but some dogs are so obsessed that medication along with a behavioral modification plan is the only combination that works. Many of these disorders occur because of a chemical imbalance in the brain. When this is the case, behavior-modifying drugs can dramatically improve the life of a dog with OCD. These drugs can be taken for life or for a limited period of time as a support to a positive behavior modification program.

Dealing with your dog's stress, fear, and phobias can be extremely challenging. Keep in mind that although these issues may sometimes be difficult to cure completely, it is possible, through the implementation of various positive training protocols, to reduce them to a manageable level. The physiological impact of stress on dogs can be significant, so it's critical to stay attuned to your dog's emotional responses and prevent any seemingly harmless quirks from developing into potentially damaging obsessions or anxieties. Always start by figuring out where, when, and why the behavior started. For more severe cases, work with your veterinarian to rule out any medical conditions, and with a reward-based training professional to help you develop an effective behavior modification program.

9

CANINE AGGRESSION

From Resource Guarding to Leash Aggression

Defining aggression is not easy, because there are so many variables associated with this highly complex behavior. But by investigating the function served by an aggressive act, we can begin to gain a better understanding. At its core, aggressive behavior addresses the dog's need to increase distance from a perceived danger and includes threat and action displays ranging from a subtle lip lift to a deep bite. In most cases the intention is not so much to harm as it is to change the "threat's" behavior by making it go away.[1]

Aggressive behavior is deeply rooted in the dog's instinctual need for safety. Growling, snapping, lunging, and biting are critical ways of communicating intent, and whether that intent is to warn, intimidate, resolve conflict, increase distance, defend, or cause harm, aggressive behavior is designed to ensure personal safety and survival. Even on an emotional level, when a dog is fearful, frustrated, angry, anxious, stressed, or in pain, safety is of paramount importance.

As discussed, some people explain all aggressive behavior in terms of dominance, but as we now know, using the "d word" is misleading. The term itself suggests that the dog has a preconceived plan to use aggression as a means of establishing elevated status; this fuels an owner's anger and encourages a rank-reduction protocol involving punishment, confrontation, and other unpleasant methods to establish an owner's authority. This in turn increases the likelihood that the dog will aggress again in the future.

Although aggressive behavior is an effective way for dogs to control their environment, affect behavior in others, ensure priority access to resources, and achieve reproductive success, explaining dogs' aggression in terms of a supposed desire to be the "alpha" grossly misinterprets the source of the aggression. A more accurate explanation is that a dog that has not been taught how to function successfully in a domestic environment will behave the only way he knows how. He may use aggression to control access to food, space, furniture, or other things that provide comfort and pleasure, but this is more likely done out of fear that he will lose access to those resources than because he wants to be "above" everyone else in the household.

So if attaining the position of "alpha" is not the root cause of domestic dogs' aggressive behavior, what is? Genetics, health, age, sex, fear, imbalance of brain chemicals, hormones, and whether the dog is intact or neutered are factors that influence aggressive behavior. Studies show, for example, that due to higher testosterone levels, intact male dogs between eighteen months and two years of age have a greater incidence of aggression than females or neutered males.[2] Dogs may also bite when in pain and for other medical reasons, but there are some cases of aggression that simply cannot be easily explained. These cases are categorized as *idiopathic* (unexplained) aggression, which manifests itself as a sudden explosion absent of any known trigger. Idiopathic aggression has been linked to chemical disturbances in the brain, such as canine epilepsy.[3]

There is a clear link between anger, anxiety, and fear-based aggressive behavior. This has recently been demonstrated by Dr. Steven Hamilton at the University of California and Dr. Karen Overall at the Center for Neurobiology and Behavior at the University of Pennsylvania. Hamilton and Overall found that dogs with a history of aggression problems have levels of neurotransmitters and stress hormones similar to those of dogs that suffer from fear and anxiety.[4] When a dog aggresses, he surpasses his stress threshold, causing his limbic system (the emotional brain) to take over as he prepares for flight or fight. When this occurs, the cerebral cortex (the thinking brain) is inhibited, explaining why it is so hard to get a reactive dog's attention and encourage him to learn: while he is aggressing, he is incapable of rational thought. A punitive trainer might respond by trying to suppress the aggressive outburst with punishment, whereas a positive trainer would immediately remove the dog from the stressor by quickly walking him away or creating some distraction to cut through the reaction. Only when the dog is in a calmer state can he begin to learn again. *The secret to successfully treating aggression is to never put your dog in a situation where he goes beyond his stress threshold.* This requires sensitive, compassionate handling and manipulation of his environment to set him up for success while working on changing the way he feels about a particular stressor.

Unfortunately, we cannot sit down with our dogs and ask them how they feel, but we can observe them closely to understand *why* they feel. We can help an aggressive dog become more confident by teaching him to see a perceived threat or potential loss of a valued resource in a different light. This is the key to successfully changing the behavior. For some dogs this can be achieved relatively quickly, but others require more time; each dog learns at a different pace. Positive reinforcement is the most effective philosophy to use in these cases, because the methods have a lasting impact, even on the "red zone" dogs.

Most owners want quick fixes for their dog's aggressive behavior because they worry about what damage their dog might do, but the "quick fix" idea demeans a dog's emotional experience and is psychologically unachievable. When a dog is suffering from anxiety or fear, professing that he can be "fixed" quickly is a dangerous idea and fundamentally wrong.

Imagine what would happen if a person who suffered from chronic fear or attacks of anxiety went to their psychotherapist and was guaranteed he would be "cured" in an hour, a day, or even a few weeks. This guarantee would be false, and that therapist wouldn't be in business for long.

A dog needs time and gentle support to change the way he feels emotionally, and even though some behavioral modification processes take more time and effort on the front end, the result is a lifetime of positively changed behavior. Punitive training suppresses the behavior without addressing the cause and changing the way the dog feels inside, so even though it may look like the dog is "behaving" better after being punished, the negative behavior will continue to occur. Continual suppression of aggressive behavior through punishment is very dangerous because every incident creates another negative experience for a dog that is already about to explode.

Unlike other manifestations of aggressive behavior, predatory aggression is not emotionally driven and is largely influenced by genetics. Some dogs find it reinforcing to chase other animals or moving objects as it fulfills an instinctive need, but this is only the beginning of the predatory sequence. Over thousands of years, humans have bred the desire to bite and kill out of the domestic dog, but occasionally a deeper instinct takes over. Although many dogs, including my Sadie, enjoy shaking and disemboweling stuffed toys, this sequence does not translate to live animals or people. Herding breeds are adept at eyeing, stalking, and chasing their "prey," but they will seldom attack and kill the animals they are herding. Dogs that are motivated by the chase, grab, bite, and kill part of the sequence can be very dangerous to live with, especially around small animals and children.

Aggressive behavior therefore serves many important functions for dogs; it is a deeply rooted natural instinct that ensures reproductive success, safety, and survival. If aggression is successful, it can be an effective way to repel a perceived threat and to control resources, space, and environment. On an emotional level, aggressive behavior is very stressful for a dog, especially if the behavior is triggered by a traumatic incident, abusive handling, or an inability to cope with continually changing environments. Regardless of origins or intent, aggression is almost never a useful or wanted behavior in any domestic environment and must be treated appropriately to preserve the well-being of the dog, his environment, and his human family.

The Limitations of "Quick Fix" Training

Angela and her daughter moved into a beautiful new home after selling the family business and desperately wanted a dog. During a trip to the local pet store, they spied Tink, an eight-week-old Basset Hound, staring at them through the store window. Angela knew the puppy came from a puppy mill but couldn't resist the cute little face that looked up at her, so without much hesitation she purchased Tink for an enormous sum of money. All went well for the first few months until Tink began to show a "stubborn" side. Concerned that her pup was getting out of control, Angela immediately contacted a trainer from a well-known training company, who put a shock collar around the pup's neck and "electrically corrected" her each time she misbehaved. Because Tink was a "naughty" little puppy, she received many such corrections, some so harsh that a small burn mark appeared on her neck. Tink finally "learned her lesson" and became very obedient, listening to everything the trainer said and complying with Angela's every wish. Angela wasn't comfortable using the shock collar, but Tink was finally becoming the obedient puppy she had always wanted.

A month after shock training started, Angela noticed that although Tink was still listening to her, she had lost her puppy vitality, becoming quiet and spending long hours asleep during the day. Angela began to worry that her dog seemed disconnected and depressed. Worse still, Tink had started to lunge and aggress toward other dogs—successfully attacking the unlucky few with whom she had come in contact. Even though Angela turned the collar to the highest setting to curb this behavior, it didn't seem to be working. She contacted the trainer again, who this time swapped the shock collar for one that sprayed Tink in the face every time she aggressed. Three thousand dollars' worth of training later, Tink was "fixed" again, and walks became more enjoyable for Angela.

However, as is common with quick fixes, they quickly come unstuck. Soon, neither shock nor spray could stop Tink's aggressing, so the trainer told Angela that in his opinion Tink was a lost cause and should be put down. Angela reluctantly agreed and scheduled a date for the euthanasia but couldn't bring herself to go through with it, so she stopped walking Tink altogether, confining her to the house and a tiny backyard. Angela didn't like that she had to keep her dog in the home, but it was the only way to ensure everyone's safety. Without exercise Tink became even more unsettled and anxious, tuning out her family completely and plunging into a nervous depression.

Angela was clearly distressed when she contacted me because she felt like she had failed her dog. As I walked up to the house and saw Tink watching me through the railings I understood why Angela had fallen in love with her. The big droopy face and huge floppy ears could not fail to melt even the hardest heart, and her sweet greeting made it difficult to think she was anything but an angel.

Even though thousands of dollars had been spent on "training," the harsh techniques had done nothing but cause significant damage. Like so many owners, Angela had taken little time to educate herself about training methods and employed a trainer from what she thought was a reputable company. But instead of focusing on basic learning skills and treating the root cause of Tink's negative behavior in a positive way, the trainer she employed taught her dog to obey through punishment and used man-made devices designed to suppress negative behavior through discomfort and pain. When this failed to put Tink "in her place," the trainer gave up, labeled her a liability, and recommended euthanasia.

It didn't take long for Angela to realize that consigning Tink to a lifetime of harmful punishment was having a detrimental effect on her dog both physically and mentally. The only thing Tink had learned so far in her short life was to fear everything. If she approached the sofa, walked on the Persian rug, ignored a command, jumped up, mouthed, toileted in the home, or lunged at a dog outside, she received a painful shock. Tink's resulting mental instability had been shaped by the harsh training she'd received, and this damaged dog had no trust in or connection with Angela at all.

Shock attempts to suppress a dog's negative behavior with static electricity and the resulting "obedience" is labeled a "success" by those who use this method. However, just because a particular behavior has been *suppressed* does not mean that the behavior has *improved*. Even though supporters of electronic shock collar training may praise its supposed effectiveness, ultimately dogs trained using shock will comply or cooperate only out of fear. Such a dog is not being obedient in the true sense of the word, but rather practicing avoidance. Shock controls a dog without allowing that dog to be given a chance to make choices and solve problems, and this often leads to learned helplessness and essentially cripples the dog's true learning ability.[5]

Proponents of shock training often claim that the method gets a bad rap due to misuse by people who don't really understand how to do it "correctly." Regardless of how high you set the dial and the timing employed when delivering the shock, the unpleasant fundamental truths about how this method truly affects an animal's behavior cannot be disputed. I've also heard trainers justify their use of shock collars by calling the training "gentle persuasion," but it's about as gentle as punching someone in the neck with a smile on your face.

I don't blame dog owners who are unaware of the negative consequences and limited results of shock training, but I do believe that anyone who wants the best for their dog should fully research the most appropriate and humane dog training methods available and understand the repercussions of punishment techniques. I know that some dog training companies and individuals have very sophisticated and deceptive sales pitches that persuade even those who instinctively *know* that shocking their dog is not the right thing to do. But I reserve my utmost disdain for those who have studied behavior enough to know the truth and still decide that it's okay to use shock and other harsh aversives.

Rehabilitating a dog that had suffered such abuse was going to be tough, but I was confident that a humane approach would go a long way toward reestablishing trust. The most difficult problem to overcome was Tink's reactivity toward other dogs. It was vital she have exercise, but her reaction was so intense, I could understand Angela's deep concerns about walking her.

Leash Aggression

Leash reactivity and aggression are exacerbated by a dog's feeling restrained and therefore unable to act naturally in a social situation. In normal circumstances, an unleashed dog could put sufficient distance between himself and a fear source. But leashed he is unable to increase distance. His only option is to react aggressively in the hope that the fear source will go away, bringing him profound relief. The more success he has with his aggressive display, the more he will use it in similar situations. In response, the owner becomes tense when walking and keeps the leash tight, transmitting nerves and fears down the leash to the dog and effectively making the behavior worse. Dog and owner are locked in a cycle of tension and leash lunging that becomes very difficult to change.

To begin Tink's rehabilitation, I concentrated on basic focus training in and out of the home, teaching her to look at and take cues from Angela while gaining confidence in different environments. Even though Angela was nervous to walk Tink outside, it was vital that she not only observe her dog's body language—to pick up any signals of heightened arousal or discomfort—but also to appear confident and provide support at all times so that Tink could learn from her. I knew that Tink's discomfort around other dogs stemmed from her lack of exposure to them when she was younger. She clearly didn't understand canine language, and this put her on the defensive whenever she encountered another dog.

Not all dogs that lunge on the leash are necessarily displaying aggression—some are simply acting out of pure frustration. I have worked with many dogs that are highly reactive on leash, but as soon as the leash relaxes or they have freedom, they greet other dogs and people appropriately and invite play. If you have a social, yet frustrated dog, simply turn and walk him away from the source until he is more composed; allow him to greet only when he is calm and the leash is loose. Some leash lungers feel more confident carrying a "security blanket"—a comforting object—when they walk. Walking with a toy in the mouth, which acts like a child's pacifier, comforts and keeps the dog relaxed.

The punishment Tink had received for lunging made her behavior even worse. Because Tink had been punished each time she reacted negatively toward an approaching dog, she began to associate the sight of other dogs with the pain of punishment. As soon as I started changing her emotional response by redirecting her focus and playing with her when she saw other dogs, her discomfort around them turned into curiosity.

The brain's circuits for aggression are separate from those for play; by playing with Tink near other dogs I was effectively engaging her play drive and shutting off any fear she felt. This increased the levels of dopamine in her brain, which not only helped her feel good but also changed the way she perceived another dog's presence. There is such a thin line between calm and fearful behavior, so I had to go carefully, gradually reducing the distance between the dogs while keeping Tink comfortable. If at any point she reacted negatively, I quietly walked her away, waited until she was in a state that allowed her to learn again, and then repeated the process.

Slowly but surely, Tink began to associate the sight of other dogs with positive things that made her feel good. The key to changing the way a dog behaves is to change how he feels. Even though the punishment she'd received in the past had suppressed her negative behavior at that moment, it had done nothing to change the way she felt emotionally, so the real problem had never been resolved.

For the first time, Tink was given the freedom to make better choices around other dogs—choices that made her feel good. The change in her behavior was almost immediate, as this broken dog became eager and motivated, walking past other dogs with no reaction at all. In fact, it seemed that she was now ready to experience her first greeting. I never like to allow insecure dogs to greet face to face to begin with, as the pressure of a facial greeting can be too stressful, so we practiced parallel walking and following other dogs until we got to the point where Tink experienced her first bottom sniff. Angela and I must have looked like a couple of madwomen as we celebrated this monumental moment, but it signified a huge breakthrough in Tink's learning process. We continued to practice "curved greetings," in which both dogs were walked toward each other in an arc rather than head on, mimicking appropriate canine greeting language. The dogs were allowed to greet for a few seconds and then moved away in opposite directions, but the face time increased with each subsequent meeting. Tink made her first friend—a trusty old male Beagle called Walter. Walking with Walter gave her confidence, and they met up daily to experience the joys of ambling together. When the time was right, we began adding other dogs to the mix and developed a regular walking group. Watching Tink play with her new buddies, I couldn't help but think what a tragedy it would have been if Angela had followed that final piece of advice from her former trainer.

Tink had suffered so much throughout her most important developmental period simply because her trainer and owner didn't understand the value of a positive learning experience. There are still people who vehemently defend electronic shock collar training, saying that when used correctly, these collars are a minor irritation but do not cause pain. Even if that were the case (and it's usually not), why resort to shock when you can get much better results with methods that motivate a dog to behave without force and without any possibility of discomfort or damage? And even if a trainer knows exactly how to operate a collar effectively, the majority of dog owners do not have this "skill." Positive reinforcement offers a wealth of great alternative methods that can dramatically modify even the most intense behaviors in our dogs. Angela experienced the power of positive reinforcement firsthand and saw how it changed her dog's life for the better as well as her own.

Back Off, It's Mine!— Resource Guarding

Caspar stood stiffly over his bowl and ate slowly with one eye on his food and the other on us. Quietly and deliberately, Caspar growled—a deep, guttural sound that clearly told us to back away. Caspar's owners couldn't understand where this guarding behavior had come from, because otherwise he was a loving, joyful animal. But as feeding time approached, Caspar became watchful and wary. So far the couple had heeded his warnings, but it was only a matter of time before a bite occurred, and with a new baby on the way, it was vital they get his behavior under control.

I have worked with many dogs that guard their resources, but Caspar, a neutered two-year-old Shepherd mix, was a particularly tough one. He had been adopted from a shelter at the age of three months and was the only pet in the household. His owners were a hard-working young couple who gave him everything he wanted, but they had noticed this guarding behavior since the first day they adopted him—a major red flag. Guarding food at such a young age indicated that, along with other contributing factors, this behavior probably had a genetic component, and I would not have been surprised if somewhere in Caspar's family tree there were other practiced resource guarders.

Caspar's owners couldn't understand why he felt the need to guard his food bowl so viciously from them. They had what they thought was a good relationship with their dog and had always been careful not to challenge him. But despite this solid relationship, Caspar continued to guard his food—a behavior relatively common among domestic dogs and usually influenced by a number of environmental and situational stimuli, including a dog's natural instinct to survive.

A dog that has primary access to food has nutritional and therefore reproductive advantage over others, and even though thousands of years of domestication have changed today's dog in many ways, instincts like this can remain deeply rooted. Because dogs have evolved from scavengers, other animals can be viewed as competitors for food, which threatens an individual's survival. In this context, guarding access to scraps becomes extremely important. Caspar was deeply insecure and saw everyone, including his owners, as a threat to a resource he valued. Food made him feel good, and the potential of losing a resource that gave him pleasure encouraged his vigilance, anger, and irritability.

Because it's difficult for people to understand why dogs guard and why there is social competition, many owners get angry and confrontational with their dogs. Yet most warm-blooded animals, including humans, guard possessions and resources that are important to them. Any "machismo" fighting or wrangling a dog into submission will just increase that dog's desire to compete. Using positive reinforcement methods instead builds up trust by changing the way a dog feels about someone's presence near resources that he values.

I began teaching Caspar by changing the physical picture, giving him a new bowl, and placing it in a different location. I then varied feeding times so that he never had the chance to become tense when his body clock told him that is was time for food.

I utilized the *empty bowl method* by picking his bowl up, pretending to fill it with kibble, then placing it on the ground in front of him. Caspar went eagerly toward it but found that is was empty. Perplexed, he looked first at his owners and then at me. As soon as he looked at me, I praised him and threw a bit of kibble into his bowl. After he had finished eating he looked at me again and was rewarded with more food. I repeated this a dozen times until all his food had been eaten. Caspar was now beginning to understand that I was becoming a positive part of his feeding experience because I was providing him with food, and my presence at his bowl also signaled that he was going to get more. I advised Caspar's owners to feed every meal to him for the following week just as I had done, so he would become comfortable while he was eating. As his behavior gradually improved, the couple began throwing in larger handfuls of kibble. Eventually they were able to place his bowl full of food on the ground and watch him eat while he remained relaxed in their presence.

During this first part of the training, the couple was to remain motionless near Caspar's bowl, because in the past, movement from them had elicited a negative reaction. So that the couple could walk past his feeding area comfortably, I taught them to pass by his empty bowl and throw a piece of chicken into it. Every time they approached his empty bowl, Caspar would run toward them, eagerly anticipating the tasty treat. Having repeated this action many times, the couple then walked by his bowl while he was eating his kibble and threw in the higher-value food. Within a month Caspar's guarding behavior had completely disappeared.

The Trade—Teaching the "Take It and Drop It" Cue

You can prevent resource guarding from developing in the first place by teaching your puppy or dog to trade and give up objects, making the whole experience a game. Giving your puppy a high-value chew toy and holding onto the other end for a short period of time while he chews will allow him to be confident about your presence near his high-value objects. People often make a guarding situation worse by being confrontational and threatening when their dogs refuse to give up an object. However, if you turn the whole process into a game of trade by teaching the "take it and drop it" game, your dog will feel good about giving up any object he has in his mouth.

STAGE ONE—THE TRADE

Start with an object of low value and present it to your dog. When he opens his mouth to take the object, say "take it."

Allow him to play with the object; then present him with a duplicate that you have behind your back. As your dog drops the object he has in his mouth, say "drop it" and reward him with the duplicate that you have in your other hand, saying "take it."

STAGE TWO—ADDING VALUE

Keep repeating this exercise; when your dog is consistently complying, you can gradually build up the value of the toy. If he doesn't want to give up the higher-value toy, walk away from him, produce a new toy, and start directing all your interest to that new toy while you play with it. Most likely his curiosity will get the better of him, and he will come over and give up the toy he has in his mouth. Immediately reward his decision by giving him the new toy and repeating the "take it," "drop it" sequence.

THE EMERGENCY "DROP IT"

If you are in a crisis situation and your dog won't give up the delicious (but dangerous) chicken bone in his mouth, you can try playing the "go find it" game. Without moving toward your dog as he is eating, start dropping small high-value treats on the ground where he can see you. Tell your dog to "go find" the treats you have dropped. Nine times out of ten, your dog will let go of whatever he has in his mouth to play the game. You can encourage this process by teaching him the game in other circumstances so that it's not only associated with when he steals something. This exercise helps lower his perception of threat, focuses his mind on something that makes him feel good, and prevents both of you from getting into a situation that could be dangerous. If you don't have high-value food available when your dog has something in his mouth, then your only alternatives are to let him eat it (and observe him closely afterward to make sure there are no bad aftereffects) or implement a major distraction, such as ringing the doorbell or getting his leash to take him on a walk. These distractions may be far more exciting than eating or holding onto whatever he has picked up.

Dogs will also guard other objects such as toys, and locations such as beds, sofas, or other valued space. If your dog is a resource guarder, you can prevent this other guarding behavior by removing objects or cutting off access to prized locations.

TIPS TO PREVENT GUARDING

- Change your dog's emotional response to something he values by teaching him to feel differently about your presence near these resources.

- Implement distractions, like ringing the doorbell or making a noise in another room, to encourage your dog to leave whatever object or location he is guarding so that you can safely remove the object or block access to the location.

- Give your dog enough outlets in his day to enrich his environment. Occupying his mind will give him something else to focus on.

- Train a conditioned response, such as the "take it" and "drop it" cues. This takes the emotion out of what can be a hard thing for dogs to do.

- Keep things predictable. Resource guarders do not like surprises.

- Avoid confrontation. Use play instead, turning competition into cooperation.

Five's a Crowd—Aggression in a Multidog Household

Judy and Louie had a soft spot for small dogs. The once happily married couple had taken in rescue dogs for many years and always enjoyed doing so until they adopted a Toy Poodle named Manny. As soon as Judy saw him, she knew she had to have the little guy, but when they brought him home, a previously calm household changed overnight. Not only was the couple's marriage suffering because of Manny's behavior, but so were their other dogs—five-year-old Lhasa Apsos, Shayna and Butch. Manny had what the couple described as a "Jekyll and Hyde" personality:

one moment he was sweet and cuddly, the next he attacked violently, especially if anyone approached Judy while he was close to her. Manny had bitten Louie on many occasions, most annoyingly when Louie tried to get into bed or sit next to his wife, but even though Judy recognized that Manny's behavior was out of control, she still made excuses for him and continued to indulge her beloved Poodle. The other dogs in the household were living under constant stress from the fighting, and Louie worried that one day all the dogs would end up getting seriously hurt.

Louie told me that this pint-sized dog had fundamentally changed the relationship between him and his wife, primarily due to his anger over Judy's steadfast refusal to ever discipline Manny for his bad behavior. Any time Louie tried to discipline the dog, it led to an argument. Judy claimed that Louie was simply jealous of the attention she gave Manny. Louie told me that he had never wanted a third dog and had even warned his wife that if she brought another dog into the house she'd have to name it "Divorce," because it would very likely end their marriage.

When people can't communicate with one another effectively or don't respect each other's opinions and needs, my job becomes infinitely more difficult. In these cases, before I can address the often significant canine problems, I must first try to figure out whether or not all the members of the household can find a way to work together. Usually I can achieve this by reminding everyone that the dog has no say in the matter and that they must act responsibly to do right by the animal. If, however, one or more members of the family are not committed to having the dog in the first place, my options as a trainer are severely limited. Luckily for Manny, Louie was eventually willing to concede that if we could turn around the behavior, he'd willingly commit to the process.

Throughout the day I witnessed Manny interact with his family, and it was clear what an utter tyrant he had become. He savagely aggressed any time Louie approached Judy on the couch or on the bed, and he regularly fought with Butch, the other male in the household, over primary access to Judy.

Conflicts in multidog households are very common. Minor disagreements are normal in canine social relationships and actually prevent violence, but major conflict can be very damaging and stressful for the entire family. Fights occur when dogs are in direct competition with each other over access to a valued resource or space, in response to persistent bullying, during moments of high arousal (such as when the doorbell rings or at the beginning of a walk), when an owner shows affection to one dog and not the other, and when one dog does not respond appropriately to another's social cues. More often than not, aggression between dogs is not a case of an upstart challenging for dominance but rather a dog that cannot tolerate or recognize appropriate signals in others. The old idea of implementing a social hierarchy in a multidog household to defuse the conflict just doesn't work.

Witnessing a fight between Manny and Butch was disturbing, but interestingly enough, even though the fight sounded terrible, both dogs emerged without a scratch. The snarling and gnashing of teeth, the growling and grabbing of fur made it look like the dogs were trying to kill each other, but in reality, both dogs seemed to be fighting *without* wanting to inflict harm— intentionally restricting the strength and intensity of their bites. This made the prognosis for a calmer household much more positive. If either dog had really wanted to cause harm, not only would they have bitten down hard or grabbed and held on, but the bites would have been purposefully delivered to parts of the body that they could disable or damage most severely, such as the legs, the belly, or the throat. I would have been a lot more concerned about their future lives together if this had been the case. I have been in many households where dogs will fight to the death, and in such situations the prospect of rehoming one of them becomes a reality. There are some dogs that are just not meant to live together, and their lives can be made much better by moving them to different households. It's not fair to make dogs that hate one another live together; the daily stress each dog experiences makes life miserable for both (and usually for the owners, too).

I advised Judy to leave Manny on the floor because even the act of picking him up made Butch angry. To build trust between the dogs and teach them restraint, Judy and Louie had to become more confident leaders in their household so that all the dogs could look to them for direction. If either dog showed signs of arousal, the offender was quietly removed for a brief time-out to calm down. All the dogs were taught new cues, including a recall and "settle" cue, so that they could be called away from their resources and directed to their specific areas for quiet time. They were also rewarded for practicing avoidance behaviors such as turning their heads and walking away from each other or backing down from a highly charged situation. The dogs were taught to follow the couple whenever they were asked—which worked well to lessen arousal levels—as well as to take turns receiving affection. While Butch was petted, Manny was placed in a "settle" until it was his turn. If tension built between them, Judy walked away from the scene, leaving the dogs by themselves. With the source of conflict gone, the dogs had nothing to fight over. If a fight did occur, Judy got up and left the fight, blowing a loud whistle that stopped the dogs in their tracks.

If disagreements are severe and stress levels are too high in an emotionally charged environment such as the home, both dogs should be taken to neutral territory where space and a new environment will allow them to learn. Giving both dogs activities in each other's presence as well as taking them for walks or doing agility training side by side helps them concentrate on doing something more positive while building up a better association with each other.

Although dogs that fight do need to be separated for safety, especially when they cannot be actively supervised, separation can also make things worse. Barriers between two dogs cause frustration, and restraining them on leashes while they are together can also exacerbate a tense situation, yet it is still vital to give each dog space and make them feel safe.

People often ask me how to break up a dog fight safely, but there is no clear answer because it all depends on the specific situation. I advise owners to avoid getting between two fighting dogs because of the risk of getting bitten and the prospect of making the situation worse, but when a fight happens, there is usually so much frantic confusion that people often forget and dive right in. Trying to restrain one or both dogs puts you at risk of becoming a target of redirected aggression because restraining a frenzied dog makes that dog feel vulnerable to attack. Imagine if someone threatening came toward you while another person held your arms back so that you couldn't defend yourself. You would probably try to get free of that person holding your arms so you could protect yourself. This is exactly the situation you put your dog in when you restrain him during a conflict. A safer way to break up a fight is to place some furniture, like a chair, between fighting dogs or to throw a coat, blanket, or sweater over their eyes. I once broke up a fight between two Pit Bulls that were hanging onto each other and refusing to let go. The only way I could get them to release was to throw my coat over their eyes, cutting off their vision. As soon as they couldn't see each other, they gave up the fight.

It's very common for dogs to protect their owners, as they naturally gravitate toward and want to protect those people who make them feel good. Manny saw the other dogs in the household and Louie as competition for Judy's attention. The family had previously consulted with a trainer, who had told them (of course!) that Manny was displaying dominance and wanted to establish himself as the head of the household. The resulting punitive treatment had only made the situation worse by amplifying the need to compete, which encouraged more conflict. There was no question that Manny was controlling environment and movement to control access to what was important to him—Judy—but he was doing so not to achieve a higher status but out of fear of losing her attention. Because Judy had reinforced his aggressive behavior by picking him up and cuddling him after he had aggressed, Manny had learned that aggressing brought him much-needed relief with her attention. That made her even more valuable to him and made Manny increasingly dependent on her.

My aim was to teach Manny valuable impulse control skills as well as improve his relationship with Louie. I wanted to show Manny that Louie's approach wasn't a threat and that there would be negative consequences if he aggressed. I knew that if Manny's aggressing meant he was removed from Judy (the very person he wanted to be close to), he would think twice about reacting in a negative manner. We began teaching in the bedroom because it was the most volatile place in the home. Judy lay on the bed with Manny, while I placed a canvas-covered crate on the floor next to her. I then asked Louie to approach his wife. As soon as Manny showed a hint of negative reaction, Judy picked him up and gently lowered him into the crate, closing the top over him. Because the dogs were never crated in this household, I wasn't concerned that Manny would build a negative association with it. I also knew that if Judy put him off the bed and onto the floor without confining him, he would most likely charge at Louie and bite him.

Each time Louie approached the bed, Manny geared up to attack, but before he could explode he was quietly lifted into the crate and ignored. Once he was calm, he was lifted out of the crate and placed back on the bed next to Judy. After about five repetitions, Manny's responses weakened, until Louie was able to approach without a reaction. The reward for a calm response was a food reward from Louie and praise and cuddles from Judy.

Following this breakthrough, we were able to progress quickly to the next level. Louie approached, handed Judy a glass of water and the remote control, and finally sat on the side of the bed next to his wife and dog for the first time ever. In a short period of time Manny had gone from a reactive, explosive dog to one that eagerly welcomed Louie's approach. The couple continued to reinforce this success, keeping the other dogs out of the bedroom until Manny was consistently welcoming. Louie was to reward Manny with treats intermittently so that the food reward could gradually be phased out, at which stage the other dogs would be reintroduced to the bedroom.

Judy and Louie worked hard with their dogs and reaped the rewards of a calmer household. Now, instead of always being with his beloved Judy, Manny was actively choosing at times to lie next to Louie—a huge step. He was finally able to relax and become a happy, confident member of the family—and fortunately for everyone, "Divorce" was never mentioned again.

The Dangers of Flooding

Cooper was a two-year-old male Boxer that aggressed severely toward other dogs. His owners, Dannee and Camille, had tried many different methods to modify Cooper's behavior, but his response got worse and worse. He lunged toward any dog that walked past him and on two occasions broke free from his leash and attacked. Dannee and Camille told me that his behavior was very different when he attended doggy day care. Cooper never fought with the dogs at day care and seemed to be relaxed and happy at the facility.

During my first visit I asked if we could go to the day care facility to see how Cooper interacted with the other dogs around him. I'm really glad I did, because I could tell right away that even though the staff assured me he enjoyed being there, I could tell that Cooper was extremely uncomfortable in that environment.

When Dannee and Camille first adopted Cooper he had actively played with other dogs in the neighborhood, but his originally easygoing demeanor changed almost overnight, and no one knew why. A medical investigation revealed that pain from an earlier leg injury might have been the cause, but I had a feeling that contrary to what we had been told, all was not well at day care. Even though some members of staff told Dannee and Camille that Cooper was never a problem, I did some nosing around and heard a different story. Cooper regularly ended up in time-outs for "being a bully." Watching him at day care, I could see how an untrained eye could have mistakenly assumed that he was coping well—it appeared that Cooper behaved better at day care than he did at home. My suspicions were confirmed, however, within the first ten seconds of viewing him in the dog room. Cooper panted and drooled as he paced up and down the room, staying close to known exits. He was so overwhelmed that he seemed to be having a complete internal meltdown, unable to display his true emotions and shutting down completely. Cooper was being flooded by what he feared.

Flooding is a behavioral therapy that is sometimes used to "cure" people or animals of certain fears and phobias. For example, flooding is regularly used to "cure" dog-aggressive dogs like Cooper by putting the dog into an enclosure with multiple strange dogs of all ages, breeds, and sizes. The idea is that even though the aggressive dog will initially be very anxious when surrounded by what he fears, his body cannot stay in this fearful state forever and he will eventually calm down. The desired result is that the stimuli or situation that the dog previously feared no longer arouses anxiety and he learns to associate a feeling of calm with the stimuli or situation. This change is expected to help him learn to change his own behavior to avoid negative consequences while realizing that no harm would come to him even in the presence of other dogs.

In some cases flooding works, but this therapy is controversial because the likelihood of failure is so high. Most dogs that are subjected to this experience are so terrified that not only do their brains shut down, but they are also rendered unable to learn. They walk around in a state of fear, trying to survive by avoiding threat and inhibiting their desire to lash out until their body gives up and they completely surrender. To the untrained human eye, it looks like a previously dog-aggressive dog has been rehabilitated and that the desire to aggress at other dogs has been eliminated.

Unfortunately, most dogs shut down in order to survive until they are released from the enclosure. Some might reach the point where they feel more relaxed while avoiding conflict and learning to show survival-ensuring deference behaviors to those that are more threatening. The problem is, when these dogs finally come out of the enclosure, they revert back to aggressing again.

Even though Cooper was uncomfortable in day care, he had learned to cope by suppressing what he truly felt. He had had a few altercations after mounting other dogs, but he knew when he was outnumbered. This indoor day care environment, however, didn't translate to life outside. Released from his flooding experience, he felt profound relief, and as soon as he left the facility, he aggressed again at other dogs walking by. For a flooding therapy to have a better chance of success, the dog has to be put in a similar situation in all environments and situations, which is virtually impossible.

That was Cooper's last day at day care. Taking him away from that environment and teaching him to be confident with other dogs outside was more important than any physical benefit he got from being at day care.

Whether flooding is used as a behavioral therapy or a dog is unintentionally exposed to an environment that floods his senses, it's important to understand the dynamics of this process and the potential positive or negative effects on the dog. A dog that attacks other dogs, whether on or off the leash in public, is very unlikely to be comfortable around other dogs in a day care environment, even if it looks like he is behaving normally.

Unchain Me! The Dangers of Tethering

Chaining or tethering dogs is a common practice in the United States, due to the common lack of fencing between properties. Even though tying a dog to a stationary object in the front yard or backyard enables the dog to be under control outside without owner supervision, a study by the American Veterinary Medical Association in 2000 reported that 17 percent of fatal attacks on humans between 1979 and 1998 were from dogs that were restrained on their property by a tether at the time of the attack.[6] Many of the victims were children who wandered up to the chained dogs to say hello and died as a result.

Tethered dogs are more likely than nontethered dogs to respond aggressively to an approaching person, even if that person is someone the dog knows, because chaining or tethering a dog for long periods of time causes immense frustration, excessive agitation, and increased anxiety and exacerbates the dog's aggressive response.[7] Owners of these dogs seem unaware of the effects of continual confinement.

Five-year-old Cheyenne Peppers was killed by her family's three Pit Bulls as she jumped on her trampoline. Two of the dogs had spent the day tied up in the yard as the adults and their friends drove their four wheelers around the property (an activity that aroused the chained dogs), while the third dog—a pregnant female—lay close by. After hours of fun, the family went inside for lunch. Little Cheyenne came out on her own to jump on the trampoline. It's believed that the pregnant female started the attack and the other dogs broke free from their tethers and joined in. The wounds on Cheyenne's body were consistent with predation and dissection. Her body had been pulled apart.

I cite this case not because these dogs were Pit Bulls. Fatalities, maulings, and bites happen with all breeds, and any dog, regardless of breed, that is tethered for long periods can explode. When a dog is chained on a property or confined with an electric or "invisible" fence, the property is still accessible to the general public—particularly to a child who may not be able to resist touching or sometimes teasing the dog. A scared or angry dog, unable to increase the distance between himself and an approaching stranger, feels he has no other option but to fight. Tethered dogs and dogs that live within the boundary of an electric "invisible" fence are also at the mercy of other animals and people that may wander onto their territory. There are numerous reports of dogs that have been stolen from these premises only to be resold and used as bait for dog fighting or as specimens for laboratory research.

Tethered dogs have limited ability to defend themselves and are at greater risk of suffering injuries after becoming tangled in their tethers. Chained dogs often pace constantly to keep themselves stimulated and are forced to lie close to where they urinate and defecate. Owners who tether their dogs are also often neglectful, providing limited food, water, and shelter and leaving their dogs out in all types of weather. Because dogs are naturally social animals, lack of social interaction can seriously damage a dog's psychological well-being, particularly if that dog spends long periods of time by himself at the end of a chain. Dogs living in this restricted torment with limited interaction experience a build-up of frustration and anger that can explode at the slightest trigger.

Electric or Invisible Fences

I was driving my daughter home from school one afternoon when a Cocker Spaniel ran out in front of my car. Fortunately I was able to avoid disaster, but the experience left my daughter and me very shaken. The dog's owner came running out of the house, reprimanding her dog and apologizing for his disobedience. She explained that an electric fence had recently been installed but her dog kept escaping even though he was wearing his collar and the fence was activated.

I am vehemently against the use of electric shock to train dogs in any scenario. I have rehabilitated countless dogs that have been physically hurt or emotionally scarred from shock training, and the experience with the Spaniel proved to me yet again how grossly inhumane and dangerous this method is. Whose fault would it have been if I had hit the dog, or if my daughter and I had been hurt or even killed trying to avoid him? Not mine, because thankfully I was driving safely and under the speed limit. I wouldn't necessarily blame the owner either, who, like millions of Americans, believe that these electric containment systems are a good idea. No, the blame should stand squarely on the shoulders of the electric fence companies who put dogs and people at risk every day by claiming that their products are safe and effective.

An electric fence is a wireless, in-ground or "invisible" fence that is installed around the perimeter of a property, creating an invisible boundary. A dog contained within the boundary of the fence wears a "shock," "remote," or "e-" collar around his neck (and sometimes around his groin or at the base of the tail) that consists of a transmitter designed to deliver a "static correction" should the dog stray too close to the boundary. Flags are placed at intervals around the perimeter as visual markers. When dogs first learn to stay within the fence they inevitably receive a series of electric shocks, which supporters of these fences claim are harmless. Of course any kind of aversive such as shock has to be relatively strong in order to be effective and while the dog may learn to quickly associate one flag or part of the property as a no-go area, his natural curiosity will inevitably lead to subsequent shocks should he get too close to other untested areas during the "learning" process.

The transmitter emits an auditory signal or tone which is usually heard by the dog as he moves closer to the boundary and signals that a shock is imminent if he proceeds. In order to avoid discomfort and pain the dog must retreat to within the safety zones of the area when he hears the tone. Electric fence companies conveniently ignore the simple fact that because dogs make an association between the tone and the shock, just hearing the tone makes them anxious. Other dogs are so traumatized after just one shock experience that a fear memory is imprinted on the brain forever. I am saddened by the dogs I've seen who now refuse to go into their yards or have suffered electrical burns from the collars the fence companies claim are "safe and humane." The case against electronic containment systems is even stronger when you consider how many dogs break through the boundary to get to something on the other side regardless of the pain they experience or because the fence has malfunctioned in some way, just like the Spaniel had done. Many of these dogs end up getting lost, run over, or picked up by Animal Control workers who regularly find these dogs wandering around the neighborhood.

Dogs contained behind electric fences tend to become more reactive and in some cases more aggressive toward strangers and even family members. A recent study found that dogs without previous aggression problems attacked family members when the system was activated.[8] Similarly, delivery people or guests can be unwilling victims of a dog's pent-up frustration. Any dog left outside for long periods of time is likely to develop a fence-running habit—barking at cars, people, or other animals as they go by—but this behavior is a lot more prevalent in dogs with an uninterrupted view. Fence running is an unhealthy activity that exacerbates frustration, irritation, and aggression and regularly becomes a fixed action pattern the dog performs in other contexts and environments, such as on a walk. I now avoid walking my dogs in certain areas of my neighborhood because while I might understand and hope that the poor animals charging towards us stay within their invisible boundary, my dogs are terrified by what looks to be an impending attack. Dogs that live within the confines of an electric fence are also at the mercy of other animals and people who may wander onto their property, and with no visible boundary, these dogs are at greater risk of being stolen. Pedigrees have a high resale value while mixed breeds are regularly stolen and used as bait in dog fighting or for medical research.

While no fence can offer 100 percent protection, a solid fence will do a much better job of keeping your dog in his yard and others out. Electric fence companies would like you to believe that their "fences" are the perfect solution for containing your dog, offering "safety, comfort, and peace of mind," but don't be fooled by clever marketing. While the idea of allowing your dog to experience more unsupervised "freedom" might be an attractive one for you, the simple truth is that electric fences rely on pain to deter dogs from escaping, and the risks of anxiety and aggression issues, theft, and increased legal liability are too high (although companies are very quiet when it comes to talking about the negative aspects of their products!). If you don't have a physical fence around your property, keep your dog inside your home and take him out for regular toilet breaks and walks or invest in a solid fence around (or smaller "dog run" within) your property. It is a much safer and more humane and effective containment option than an electric fence will ever be.

Assessing a Dog Bite

If your dog has ever bitten in any circumstance, it is vital to find the cause and manage the situation so that you never put your dog in the position where he could bite again. This is easier said than done, especially for dogs that are serial biters, but your number one priority should be to keep other people and animals safe by managing your dog's environment 100 percent of the time.

Many people are bitten because they don't understand canine body language and misinterpret a dog's signals and intentions. This was publicly demonstrated by a notorious bite incident on live television. An Argentinian Mastiff (Dogo Argentino) named Max had been brought onto a Denver-area morning news show the day after he had been pulled from a freezing reservoir. The big dog sat by his owner and the fireman who had rescued him while veteran news anchor and longtime animal lover Kyle Dyer conducted the interview crouched next to Max, massaging his face. Throughout the segment Max gave Dyer many signals to back away, including averting his eyes, turning his head away, showing his teeth, licking his lips, and yawning, all of which demonstrated that he was stressed by her close proximity and handling. Dyer, however, through no fault of her own, didn't understand the clear signals Max was giving, and as she leaned in to give him a kiss, he bit her in the face. Dyer underwent two reconstructive surgeries, a skin graft, and ninety stitches to repair the damage done to her lip.

The story grabbed headlines throughout the United States because it so perfectly illustrated what people should never do around dogs, particularly those they do not know. What was also interesting about this case was *how* Max delivered the bite. Even though he caused a lot of damage, the quick contact he made with Dyer's face followed by an immediate release was an inhibited bite with the intention to increase distance and not to disable. If Max had really wanted to harm Dyer he could have taken her face off. It may sound strange to say that this bite was inhibited when so much damage was done, but a quick bite and release from a large dog like Max can still do a lot of harm, particularly on such a tender part of the body. If Max had intended to harm her more significantly, he could have applied more pressure to her face and bitten down harder. He might even have gone to the next level: to hold onto her face and shake it.

I agreed that Max should not be euthanized because he wasn't a danger to society. The poor dog had suffered major trauma just one day earlier and was put in a compromised position during the interview with no means of escape. Even though Max signaled his distress, his language went unrecognized, and he used the only option he had left. In a later interview Dyer spoke about the incident, saying that she had always considered herself a "dog person." She had lived with dogs all her life and had assumed that Max was enjoying being stroked and massaged. To her credit, even after suffering a horrific facial injury, Dyer acknowledged that it was a freak accident, that she was ultimately to blame for being too close, and that although many of us think we know what dogs are saying, it's clear that many times we do not. Good dog trainers do know, which is why I respect Dyer so much for helping us spread this important knowledge.

Because of the care I take when working with aggressive dogs, I have never had my skin punctured by a bite. Aggressive dogs are under stress, so I work gently and carefully with them. It may not always make for the sexiest television, but you will never see me fight or grapple an aggressive dog into submission. If a dog I was working with were to bite me or anyone else, it would be a massive failure on my part because it would mean I had lost the dog's trust and respect, and (more important) the biting behavior would become even more ingrained thanks to that experience, putting owners and the general public at greater risk of being bitten. Perhaps that's why some people mistakenly think that I don't work with aggressive dogs on my show—because they never see me battle a dog into submission. Sadly, I recognize that it may be impressive for some to watch a trainer dominate a dog while getting bitten in the process. These kinds of trainers show the scars from their previous canine battles like some sort of badge of honor, but for those of us who know how much stress these dogs are being put through during the "training" process, and understand the increased likelihood for them to bite again following such a traumatic experience, it is the height of ignorance and irresponsibility.

Vicious Dog Attacks and Fatalities

On February 28, 2010, Ashlynn Anderson was playing in her backyard when she was fatally attacked by her stepfather's dog. Ashlynn sustained severe injuries to her throat and later died in the hospital. The dog was quickly euthanized, and the resulting investigation classified the death as a tragic accident. Ashlynn's parents and grandparents live in torment over the loss of their beloved child, in part because it was a tragedy that could have been prevented. Even though attacks of this nature are rare in proportion to the number of owned dogs in this country, one fatality like this is one too many.

As a mother and a dog trainer I am dedicated to raising awareness about responsible pet ownership and prevention of dog bites. My public platforms allow me to shine a spotlight on the issue, and members of my Dog Bite Prevention Task Force (composed of veterinarians, lawyers, canine bite investigators, and pediatric surgeons) are each doing what they can to educate the public about how to be safe around dogs. In addition to working on much-needed national campaigns with the Task Force, I spend a lot of my free time teaching bite prevention to children. As the canine population continues to grow, so have the number of dog bites both in Britain and the United States. Over the ten-year period ending in 2012, the number of reported dog bites requiring medical treatment increased by 50 percent in England and 150 percent in Scotland.[9] According to a report by the U.S. Agency for Healthcare Research and Quality, the number of hospital admissions caused by dog bites in the United States nearly doubled over a sixteen-year period, increasing from 5,100 in 1993 to 9,500 in 2008.[10] And as if these numbers weren't bad enough, according to 2010 statistics, there were approximately 4.5 million reported dog bites in the United States, 800,000 of which were serious enough to require medical attention.[11]

Even though statistics can be misleading, there is no question that hospital admissions from dog bites are increasing. This is alarming but not altogether surprising, considering how popular dogs have become. For the first time, according to the latest census, dogs outnumber children in American households.[12] Most of these dogs are privileged members of the family with nothing more to do than lie on the couch all day. Unfortunately, more "unemployed" dogs means more bored animals who consequently suffer stress and anxiety. Most dogs receive no formal training, but for those that are taken to class and are trained using punitive, outdated methods, an increase in negative behavior is often the result.

Several other factors are exacerbating the dog bite problem, and first among these are the poor breeding practices used by the puppy mill industry and backyard breeders. Puppy farmers care very little for the well-being of the dogs they breed; they are more interested in simply making money by churning out puppies, with no attempt to breed for good temperament and no effort to socialize their puppies with humans or other animals. Such lack of socialization causes fear and insecurity—leading causes of aggressive behavior. A large portion of the blame for these incidents rests with the irresponsible owners who use their large breed dogs for protection and intimidation without adequately socializing them. Finally, intact male dogs make up a significant majority of the pool of dogs who have attacked in the past—yet another reason why intransigent owners should overcome their reluctance to have their dogs neutered.

Contrary to the reports that usually accompany these incidents, the majority of such attacks do not come out of the blue. There are a plethora of markers and flags before an attack occurs that go unnoticed or are ignored. In many cases dogs that have attacked viciously have been actively encouraged to be aggressive by their owners. This is one of many reasons why I do not agree with breed-specific legislation—that is, laws that restrict or ban ownership of certain breeds of dogs, like the Pit Bull Terrier. I am well aware that the majority of serious attacks come from large breeds, but I am also acutely aware that for all the reasons just detailed, the majority of these attacks could have been prevented if owners took more responsibility for the care and welfare of their dogs. What's more, any breed of dog can bite and cause significant damage (especially to vulnerable parts of the body), just as any breed of dog can make a good family pet.

While investigating the more serious maulings and dog-related fatalities, I started to notice a trend. Many of the attacks, particularly on children, came from dogs that were known to the children but did not live with them full time. The child victim was very often found to be either visiting an extended family member or living between two parents, as was the case with little Ashlynn. Sometimes the dog was staying with the victim's family while the owners were away. The frequency of this unfamiliar-dog-or-child trigger in fatal dog attacks must be accounted for by our society as we develop greater awareness about how potentially dangerous dogs are likely to react when placed near unfamiliar people or in unfamiliar environments.

Most attacks on infants occur within a few months of birth or when the parent or guardian leaves their infant in an area the dog values, such as the parents' bed that at one time had also been shared by the dog. Many dogs that kill also have a history of aggressive response and high prey drive. I understand why people want to euthanize these dogs so quickly after an attack, but I also think it's important that canine behavior professionals are brought in to investigate the circumstances of these fatalities. Such quick euthanasia eliminates the most critical piece of evidence from the event, which might otherwise have provided valuable insight into why the attack occurred. Only by understanding how, when, where, and why these attacks happen can we increase our chances as a society of saving lives in the future.

Jim Crosby, a former canine police officer, certified behavior consultant, and canine aggression expert, has regularly consulted on serious attacks and has examined many dogs that have killed people. According to Crosby, the rising bite numbers indicate that a large part of this problem lies with those irresponsible owners who choose not to spay and neuter, who chain their animals outside for extended periods, and who ultimately care less about their animals than they should. I wholeheartedly agree when he says that, more often than not, it's the two-legged animals more often than the four-legged ones that precipitate the problem.[13]

These deaths are extremely rare, but dog bites are not. The Humane Society of the United States reports that 50 percent of children will be bitten by a dog before their twelfth birthday.[14] Children under the age of five are most likely to be bitten, and most of these bites come from a dog that the child knows (usually the family dog or that of a relative or friend). Children are most likely to be bitten in the face, as they are closer to a dog's eye level, making it easier for a dog to feel threatened by eye-to-eye contact. Children love to kiss and hug dogs, even though these expressions of affection do not translate well in the dog world. Fast movements can also stimulate a dog's prey drive and/or chase instinct, and higher-pitched voices can sometimes startle a dog and make him fearful. A dog can be frustrated by rough play or by teasing, and a child can inadvertently inflict pain by pulling a tail or poking an eye. It is also hard for children to read and understand a dog's body language, so they miss vital signals that could alert them to get out of harm's way. Parents and guardians also frequently miss these signals, but even in some cases where the grownups are aware of their dog's aggressive history, little is done to address the dog's behavior. Most people simply believe that such tragedies will never happen to them.

The only way to keep young children completely safe around dogs is for parents and guardians to be responsible for their dogs at all times and to teach their children how to behave not just with their dog, but also around other dogs with whom they might come in contact. An infant or young child should *never* be left unsupervised with *any* dog at *any* time, and *all* interactions between them need to be actively supervised. If this isn't possible, the child and dog need to be safely separated so that no interaction can occur between them. According to a number of pediatric surgeons I have interviewed, dogs should never be allowed to sleep with a child, because some of the worst bites they see happen when a sleeping dog has been awakened suddenly, by the child either knowingly waking the dog up or accidently rolling into him while they are sleeping.[15] All dogs need to receive a humane canine education to help them live successfully in a domestic situation, and if a dog is showing worrying behavior, the owner should seek help from a qualified professional.

As awareness spreads and people take more responsibility for their pets, one can only hope that the alarming rise in dog bite statistics in the United States will begin to trend downward. Until this happens, though, the future doesn't look bright, and more people will find their lives changed forever because of a bite that in most cases could have been prevented.

Assessing Future Risk

If your dog has bitten and you are worried he will bite again, contact a positive reinforcement training professional to help you work with the behavior and assess future risk. Be prepared for a prognosis that may not be very good if your dog has a long history and very low threshold for aggressive response, or if bite incidents have become more severe and frequent. If you cannot successfully redirect your dog's aggressive response, or the behavior has become more unpredictable and is occurring in many different situations, you have cause for concern. I am continually amazed when I see family members living with a dog that terrifies them just because one member of the household refuses to work with or rehome that dog. Successful modification for aggressive behavior relies on owner compliance, and people who are unwilling to work with their dogs endanger not only their pet's life, but also the lives of those around them.

If bite injuries cause slight bruising or minimal wounds, if the behavior has only recently begun, or if a dog has a higher threshold (which makes an aggressive response more predictable), the chance of success is higher.

Ultimately, when an owner is dedicated to finding a solution to the problem using force-free methods, most dogs' aggressive response can be successfully managed as long as all members of the household are willing to devote enough time, commitment, and patience to their dog's rehabilitation.

10

SOLVING COMMON BEHAVIOR PROBLEMS

Stealing, Running Away,
Jumping Up, Barking, Leash Pulling,
Eating Poop, and Mouthing

Jumping on people, barking at the mailman, dashing out of the door, and stealing food are all very common behaviors that pet owners experience with their canine family members. What dog can resist stealing the cupcakes off the kitchen counter or suppress the desire to jump on someone coming through the door? Even if an impulsive act puts a dog in danger or causes harm to others, impulsive dogs do not consider the consequences of their physical or emotional behavior.

Just like teenagers, who tend to take more risks and have more emotional outbursts than adults, puppies and adolescent dogs find it more difficult to control themselves physically and emotionally. I cannot overstate the importance of teaching all dogs impulse control from an early age and encouraging emotional stability, because self-control often represents the fine line between a dog being surrendered to a shelter or staying in the home. Living with an impulsive dog can be very frustrating, but fortunately there are powerful positive solutions that can put an end to many types of annoying behaviors.

Stealing

I was contacted recently by a client who had had enough of her dog stealing food whenever her back was turned. To fix the problem, the lady had purchased two "scat mats"—electrified mats that she placed on the kitchen counters to give her dog a shock each time he attempted to jump up. The dog received such a jolt when he attempted to counter-surf that he squealed and ran out of the kitchen. The scat mats seemed to have done the trick, and the lady was pleased with the result, but this "success" created complications that made it relatively short-lived. The only entrance to the backyard was through the kitchen, but now, because the shock the dog had received had been so traumatic, he refused to go anywhere near the kitchen area and started having toileting accidents inside the home. A counter-surfing issue had now turned into major anxiety (and a major mess), and it took a long time before the dog felt comfortable enough to walk through the kitchen again to get to the backyard. I wish I had been contacted earlier because there are many successful nonaversive techniques to stop a dog from stealing food.

Put yourself in your dog's paws and place your favorite food on the counter when you're hungry. Now walk past and see if you can resist taking a bite. Most people who have difficulty controlling themselves around food expect their dogs to somehow resist temptation even when food is placed right in front of them. It is much more realistic to use a combination of management and training techniques to make it easy for your dog to avoid temptation while ensuring her safety. Dogs do not share our human sense of right and wrong, and if you make the mistake of leaving food on the counter where a dog can reach it, you are reinforcing her success. Blocking access to places where food is left out by using baby gates or putting the dog in another room when you have company means that there is no opportunity for your dog to fail. If this is not a realistic option, you can try tethering your dog to you so that she is with you at all times—or, if you are working in the kitchen and unable to use a baby gate, draw an imaginary line along the floor and teach your dog to stay behind that line. To do this, you need to first teach a reliable stay cue so your dog understands what is expected of her. If she crosses over the line, gently block her with your body until she goes behind the line again. If you reward her at intervals while she stays put, she will see this area as a good place to be.

Because counter surfing happens mostly when a person is not around (dogs are smart!), you can try catching your dog in the act by following these easy steps:

- Put some food on the counter and then walk away to a place where you can see the food but your dog thinks she is not being watched.

- Pick up a magazine or pretend to be doing something else so that she thinks you're not paying attention to her.

- Wait for her to go up to the counter, and just before she jumps, ask her to "leave it."

- If she backs away, praise her.

- If she takes the food, calmly remove what is left and repeat the process, putting the food in a less accessible place to make it harder for her to reach it. When she is responding well, gradually move the food back to the previous location.

- Start this exercise using low-value food before making it more difficult with the yummy stuff.

While you're entertaining guests, give your dog something else to focus on—an interactive toy such as a treat ball or a rubber toy filled with food. This activity will most likely tire her out while filling her up and quenching any desire to seek out more food. In this way, you leave your dog satisfied and your food safe!

There are obvious dangers when dogs steal food, including the potential for ingesting plastic wrapping or actual food that could be harmful, including grapes, raisins, chicken bones, and chocolate. When I was a child, my grandmother's Beagles ate all my chocolate Easter eggs three years in a row. Why I didn't learn after the first year to put them out of harm's way I don't know, but fortunately, even though I missed out on a few extra calories, the dogs survived their chocolate binges thanks to numerous trips to the veterinarian. Chocolate contains a substance called theobromine, an alkaloid of the cacao plant, which can cause cardiac arrhythmias, seizures, internal bleeding, heart attacks, and even death. The Beagles were lucky to be alive but continued their thievery and regularly stole other kinds of food from underneath my increasingly frustrated grandmother's nose. Once in a while, when they were caught in the act, a battle royal ensued as my grandmother tried to get the stolen food out of their mouths. The dogs snarled at her as she tried in vain to pry open their jaws, and as she got angrier, the dogs snarled louder. My grandmother inevitably lost the battle for fear of being bitten, and the dogs skulked away, defensive but victorious. I wish I'd known then what I know now so that I could have taught my grandmother a safer and more effective way of getting food from her dogs!

The Leave It Cue

Learning basic compliance cues that encourage impulse control is the first step toward being able to address more significant behavior issues. If you haven't built up a common language and aren't able to communicate what you want to your dog, it's silly to assume that she'll care about or be able to understand what you're asking her to do when she's jumping, chewing, running away, pulling, or barking.

Because of this, the "leave it" cue is invaluable in many situations. The "it" in question might be food that has fallen on the floor, something your dog picks up on a walk, another dog, or even a child. Here's how you help your dog learn it

STAGE ONE

- Hold a piece of food in your fingers, leaving only a little bit sticking out so that your dog does not have easy access to it.
- Extend the food toward your dog's nose and let her work out how she is going to get it out of your hand.
- She may try smelling, nibbling, or pawing at it, but don't give it to her until she hesitates momentarily, either by stopping and moving her nose back or by turning her head away.
- When she makes any motion to pull himself back, praise her and give her the food that you have in your hand.
- Repeat this exercise a couple of times until she consistently makes the decision to take her nose away from the food.

STAGE TWO

- Now add the words "leave it" while she is in the act of moving her head away. This will build up an association between the cue and the action.

- Repeat this process a number of times.
- Once she is responding reliably, ask her to "leave it" as soon as you present your hand to her; then reward her for complying.

STAGE THREE

Now that you have built up an association with the word and the action, you can make it harder for your dog.

- Put the food on your open palm so that she can see and smell it.
- Place a food reward in your other hand and hide it behind your back.
- Show your dog the food in your open palm and ask her to "leave it." At this stage it may be harder for your dog to comply because now she can actually see the treat right in front of her.
- If she tries to get it, cup your hand over the treat and place your hand behind you for a few seconds, saying the words "uh-oh" as you do this. This is called a *no reward marker* and tells your dog that she will not be rewarded for her noncompliance.
- If your dog does comply, do not reward her with the treat from the hand that you have asked her to leave. Give her the food reward that you are holding in your other hand. At this stage it's essential thats she never gets the food or object that she has decided to leave, so the reward now has to come from elsewhere.

STAGE FOUR

Up the ante by making it even harder for your dog.

- Put the food on a table or the floor.
- Repeat the process, rewarding your dog with a treat in your hand, not the one on the table or floor.

STAGE FIVE

- Put a leash on your dog and walk her past the treat on the floor.
- If she reaches for it, say "leave it" without jerking the leash, and praise and reward her for her compliance. If she grabs the treat, don't try to get it out of her mouth. Go back to the previous stage where she was successful and build up the cue until she is ready to try again.

STAGE SIX

- Keep repeating the exercise by placing other objects on the floor—preferably the types of things you want her to leave alone. Once your dog is doing well with this cue inside the home, you can start to use it outside.

The Great Escape—Hound Houdinis

Linda Quinn tearfully described to me how Buddy kept running away. Every time she opened the front door to let someone in, the Jack Russell Terrier made his escape, running over the road and into the woods beyond. The sound of the doorbell always triggered great excitement because for Buddy this meant freedom! Even if Linda held onto him, he wriggled out of her grip like a slippery eel and dashed out the door like a rocket.

As I approached the house, I braced myself to catch him, but he was too quick for me, and I joined Linda in the chase before Buddy disappeared into the woods. I make it a rule never to run after a dog if it runs away because doing so only makes the dog run faster, but in this circumstance we had to get Buddy back before he was hurt. Linda finally cornered him and carried him home. "At least," she gasped, "he keeps me fit."

Door dashing is a very common behavior with obviously dangerous consequences. Buddy was lucky that he had escaped injury thus far, but it was only a matter of time before he got seriously hurt, and Linda desperately needed help to get his dangerous habit under control.

The first step when teaching a dog not to escape is to find out why she wants to run away in the first place. Escaping not only relieves a dog's boredom but allows dogs with high prey drive to fulfill their deep-rooted need to seek out prey. Buddy was walked three times a day, but because the family didn't have a fenced-in yard, he was never off leash outside. The nature of his walk was whimsically determined by whichever direction the family wanted to take and the pace at which they wanted to walk, so he never had the freedom to do what he wanted. Buddy was living as most domestic dogs do, in a sensory-deprived environment, so the promise of fun and excitement outside the home was too much for him to ignore. Escaping made him feel good.

It was time to teach Buddy some impulse control. He was a relatively young dog who had boundless energy but had never been taught how to self-inhibit and couldn't stay still in one place unless he was sleeping. Teaching him the "stay" cue in front of an open door was no easy task. To begin with, I asked Buddy to "stay" by putting my hand up in front of my body with my palm facing him and holding it there for a moment before I gave him a food reward for complying. Once I had his focus, I gradually lengthened the time that my hand was still until I had him staying in one spot for a full two minutes—a miracle! Then I added the word "stay" and took a step back. Immediately, Buddy moved to follow me, but I lured him back to his original waiting place and repeated the exercise. This time Buddy stayed in one place and did not move a muscle until I released him—a testament to how intent he was on getting his reward. After a few more repetitions and gradually increased distance, I was able to walk to the door.

The real test came when I put my hand on the door handle and rattled it, a physical and auditory cue that the door was about to be opened, but Buddy never moved. He was doing so well that I was able to progress quickly to the next level, which involved opening the door a tiny crack and then widening it until the front door was completely open. Buddy soon learned that the decision he made to stay in one place would be rewarded, and because he loved food, his reward was thankfully more motivating for him than running away.

I then added the trigger that signaled a door dashing opportunity was imminent—the doorbell. It's one thing for a dog to sit and wait by a door during a calm teaching session, but quite another to use self-control after the doorbell has rung, seemingly out of the blue. As soon as Buddy heard the doorbell ring he ran to the door and barked excitedly. Saying nothing, I waited patiently for a moment of calm, lured him back to his spot, and then asked him to stay. The reward for his compliance was twofold—food and the opportunity to greet whoever came through the door.

In addition to impulse control training and increased outdoor activities, I made sure Buddy had enough physical and mental stimulation in the home throughout the day. I encouraged the family to play hide-and-seek games with him by hiding food around the home and sending him off to track it down. I set up some tunnels in the kids' playroom so that he could search for the squeaky toys I laid out for him at intervals "underground." Keeping him entertained in this way meant that he was much more content to stay indoors.

By the time I left the family, Buddy was staying consistently by the door when it was opened. It proved to them that even a Terrier could be taught impulse control around an exciting stimulus. I was confident that the family would keep reinforcing the teaching so that Buddy would never feel the temptation to escape again.

Teaching the Stay Cue

The "stay" cue teaches a dog impulse control skills and can be used in a variety of situations, such as at the front door, before crossing a road, and when people come into your home. Here's how you do it.

STAGE ONE—BUILDING DURATION

- Start the process by putting your hand in front of you with the palm facing your dog and hold it there for a few seconds.
- Reward your dog's attention and stillness with a treat paired with a reward word (such as the classic "good girl").
- Repeat the action and add the word "stay" as you put your hand up.
- Hold it there for a few seconds, then praise your dog, followed by a food reward.
- Once you have your dog's focus, gradually lengthen the time that your hand is still until she is staying in one spot for one minute.

STAGE TWO—ADD DISTANCE

- Ask your dog to stay and take a step back.
- If your dog moves, lure her back to the original waiting place and repeat the exercise.
- If your dog stays in one place, walk back to her and reward with the verbal praise and a treat.
- Repeat this process a number of times until your dog is consistently staying in one place; only then, increase the amount of steps you take backward until you can walk at least five steps away and back to her without her moving.

STAGE THREE—INCREASE DISTANCE

Repeat the first two steps while gradually increasing distance. Don't go too far too fast, but if your dog is responding well, you can make the distance as far as you want. If she breaks her stay at any point, go back to the previous distance and build up gradually. At this stage you are still facing her while backing away.

STAGE FOUR—VARY YOUR BODY POSITION

Dogs like to follow us when we walk away from them, so as soon as you ask your dog to stay and turn your back on her, she is likely to forget everything she has learned and follow you. That is why it is important to practice the "stay" by turning your body and walking away from your dog as well as walking to her side or around her in a circle.

STAGE FIVE—PROOFING THE STAY CUE

Can your dog stay in one place while toys are being thrown around her, when people run past, when the doorbell rings, or if you go out of sight? Verifying all of this is called *proofing* a behavior. When any learned behavior is taken to a more stimulating environment or situation, it makes it a lot harder for a dog to comply, but every dog can get to this point with reinforcement.

Jumping Up

Most dogs jump on people through sheer excitement and because it is an effective means of getting attention, but some dogs jump because they feel uneasy when someone new comes into the home and the action of jumping is an effective way to cope with that discomfort.

The best way to stop your dog from jumping up is to ignore her while she is in the act of jumping.

- Turn your back on your dog each time she jumps up at you.
- Do not look at, talk to, or touch her while she is jumping and fold your arms in front of you so that you become boring.
- When she stops jumping, wait for three seconds of four paws on the floor and then reward her with your attention.
- If she jumps again, repeat the exercise.
- Practice this with friends and family members as well so that your dog learns through consistency.

During this training process, you may find that your dog jumps even higher to get your attention. This is known as an *extinction burst*. Because the behavior that previously got your attention no longer works, your dog might try even harder to get what she desires. Be sure to persevere with the technique at this point, because she will eventually give up.

If your dog jumps on guests in excitement or as a default behavior to cope with the discomfort she feels, manage your environment by putting her in another room or keeping her behind a baby gate until she is calm. Then walk her up to your guests and teach her to greet appropriately by sitting in front of them instead of jumping. This channels her energy by giving her something to do while greeting, and a dog that is sitting cannot jump up—a development your guests will surely appreciate!

Barking

I left the house with my ears ringing, relieved to be outside in the relative calm of a hot summer day. Cars roared by as I stood on the side of the busy main road, but the noise was nothing compared to what I had just experienced. I looked at the handheld decibel meter (a device that measures the level of noise) I was carrying, not believing what I had heard and seen. The readings had gone off the charts, peaking at over 110 decibels—as loud as a jet plane taking off or a jackhammer digging next to a person's ear. One minute of exposure to that level of noise causes hearing damage, and fifteen minutes of continual exposure causes permanent hearing loss. I had been in the home for over an hour and felt like I had just emerged from a rock concert.

Barking is not only an important method of communication but also an expression and measure of a dog's emotional state. Dogs that bark excessively cause big problems for their owners and their neighbors—problems so severe that occasionally people resort to drastic measures such as devocalizing (surgically removing part of a dog's vocal cords—commonly called *debarking*). The idea of devocalizing is appalling to most people, but the surgery is performed more than veterinarians would like to admit. The couple I had just met were seriously considering this option for their four dogs.

Because humans like quick fixes, modern-day technology has unfortunately provided them with various electronic tools to suppress barking behavior. Antibark collars that emit a shock, spray, or uncomfortable auditory tone each time a dog barks promise quick solutions to a nuisance behavior, but of course, as with all such devices, they never address the reason why the dog is barking in the first place. Even beyond the issue of inhumane treatment, this means they also don't work very well. Because barking is so closely linked to emotion, suppressing the behavior with these devices or punishing the dog in a harsh and forceful way may suppress the act of barking for a period of time, but it serves only to make the underlying emotion even stronger and more resistant to change. I have seen clients in multidog households use antibark collars on one of their dogs, only to find that if another dog barks near the dog wearing the collar, the collared dog will get a spray in the face even though she never uttered a sound. Other clients have observed that their dogs learned to ignore the spray, barking until the spray reservoir was empty.

Dogs bark for many reasons, including but not limited to the following:

- To warn others that something or someone is approaching
- To identify who they are
- In response to other dogs that they see or hear
- To establish social contact
- To demand something from a person or another dog
- As an expression of fear, anxiety, or stress
- To relieve boredom or frustration
- As an expression of excitement
- During play
- To warn a perceived threat to back away

Understanding why dogs bark can help you modify a behavior that might otherwise become a significant nuisance. Watching how a dog barks by observing her body language helps identify the cause; the pitch and intensity of a bark reflects intention and emotional state. If a dog is anxious or stressed, the bark tends to be more repetitive and high-pitched, increasing in pitch and speed as the dog gets more anxious, just as we raise our voices when we are stressed. The body is usually very tense. A warning bark tends to be slower and lower in pitch, with a taut body that leans forward in a defensive posture. A dog that is barking through boredom tends to bark with the same tone for long periods.

Whatever the reason, if your dog's barking has become excessive, finding the cause is the first step in determining the best way to modify it. In general, the best prescription for most barking issues—regardless of the cause—is increased exercise and mental stimulation, which helps refocus a dog's mind and tire her out. The modern dog leads a relatively unstimulating life in the domestic home, with nothing more to do than eat two meals a day, sleep on the couch, and go for the occasional walk. This is especially hard on working breeds, which are particularly likely to bark to relieve their boredom.

The house I had just emerged from belonged to Jessie and JoAnn, who volunteered for a local rescue group and had adopted their four dogs over the course of a year. Because they both had busy lives and exhausting work schedules, the dogs spent most of their day locked up in crates, so boredom and frustration was taking its toll on all of them. I had to question the couple's decision to adopt so many dogs when they had so little time to give them, but these dogs had been on death row and it was a decision that had to be made quickly. Having lived with the noise for so long, Jessie was now hard of hearing, particularly in his right ear. He had threatened to move out if the situation didn't improve. JoAnn had talked Jessie into the adoptions, but it was a decision that he was now regretting. She refused to rehome any of her dogs and told her husband that if she had to choose between him and the dogs, she would choose the dogs. For a couple that had been married a little over two years, this was a sad state of affairs.

Bailey—an energetic but anxious Pit Bull mix—had been the first to arrive, and because of a past history of abuse, he formed an almost desperate attachment to his owners. He needed continual attention and barked until he got it. In fact, it was probably Bailey that had caused the hearing loss in his owner's right ear, because his crate was located to the right of Jessie's chair in the living room. The couple had inadvertently made Bailey's barking worse by shouting at him to stop. However, when I taught them to ignore the barking but reward the quiet with attention and play time, they saw how effective this technique was. Bailey quickly learned that he only received his family's attention when he was quiet.

Some scientists believe that dogs who live together imitate each other's sound patterns. Whether this is always true or not, it was definitely the case in this household. All the dogs barked with matching excitement before going for a walk, which made this training even harder, because the couple had a fixed pattern of predeparture cues that told the dogs a walk was imminent long before the leashes were picked up. I advised them to change their departure cues as much as they could. If the dogs barked when the couple went to get the leashes, for example, the leashes were put back and the couple sat down. If they managed to successfully attach the leashes but barking erupted as the dogs went outside, they immediately came back in until the dogs were quiet.

This technique worked well in this instance because once one of the dogs started to bark, the others joined in, but this process can be made more complicated when only one dog barks while the others remain silent. Bringing the barking dog back inside while the quiet ones stay outside is fine if you have two people doing the walking, but if you are by yourself, this problem becomes a lot trickier to deal with. In such instances, I do this technique with each dog individually, working the others back into the group once they are consistently being quiet individually. This requires patience because it means that, at least in the beginning, the dogs have to be leashed and walked separately—something that requires time and some good home management. The beauty of these teaching techniques is that they do not require any verbal communication with a dog whatsoever. In highly charged situations like these, shouting at the dog only sounds like you are joining in the conversation, so body language is much more effective and will do the talking for you.

Each of the four dogs in this household needed an outlet that was specifically designed to motivate that dog and serve its particular needs. Because Bailey loved to play with balls, he was given two half-hour daily play sessions in the backyard as well as an hour a week learning the sport of Treibball at a local dog training center. German Shepherd mix Max loved to chase squirrels and excelled at the sport of lure coursing. Boston Terrier/Bulldog mix Eve loved to chew and disembowel toys, but because of a medical condition was unable to exercise with the others. I gave the couple a selection of dog puzzles through which Eve could be fed, keeping her engaged and quiet for hours. She was also taken for daily rides in the car, as she loved to stick her head out of the window and feel the wind in her ears. Their fourth dog, Blaze, showed a real talent for finding hidden food and toys; this was further reinforced at a weekly scent work class that gave him the perfect outlet and allowed him to socialize with other dogs outside the home.

One effective method to stop a barking dog is to actually encourage that dog to bark and then teach her to stop on cue. This is called the *controlled barking* technique and can be achieved in the following way:

- Start by encouraging your dog to bark. You can use your dog's normal triggers to do this (ringing the doorbell, for example). Reward your dog while she is actively barking by giving her a treat or toy.

- While your dog's mouth is occupied chewing on the treat or by the toy, say "quiet" paired with a hand signal. If your dog is quiet for even a few seconds, reward her with another treat or game with the toy.

- Repeat this process a number of times, rewarding both the barking and the quiet.

- After a few repetitions, encourage your dog to bark again, only this time put a vocal cue to the act of barking, such as "speak," but do not give her a reward. Ask her to "quiet" and give her the treat or toy only if she complies. Now being quiet is more reinforcing than barking, because the quiet is the only behavior that earns the reward.

- Your dog has now learned two cues. "Speak" means bark and "quiet" means stop barking. Having both these behaviors on cue will really help you positively control your dog's barking habit.

All of Jessie and JoAnn's dogs required regular walks, and all of them were fed through activity toys at mealtimes rather than just from their bowls. Working for their food stimulated their brains and tired them out. Complementary therapies—such as soft music from my Canine Noise Phobia Series' *Calming* CD (see Resources), weekly massage sessions, and a dog-appeasing pheromone plug-in—helped ease what had previously been a very stressful environment in which to live.

My experience with this family proved to me that if barking this extreme could be modified by taking the steps I've described, then any barking issue can be tackled. Living with a barking dog is frustrating, but with time, thought, and effort, this behavior can be treated successfully without having to resort to punishment or surgery.

Leash Pulling

Contrary to popular belief, dogs that pull on the leash while being walked do not want to be pack leader, top dog, alpha, or dominant over their human. There is a much simpler explanation: dogs love to be outside, and the walk is a stimulating and exciting part of their day, so the desire to push ahead is very strong. From the dog's point of view, humans don't make ideal walking partners either because a dog's natural and comfortable walking pace is generally much faster than ours. Having to walk calmly by a person's side when the only thing the dog really wants to do is run and investigate the environment around her requires a degree of self-control that can be very difficult for some dogs to master. A leash, though vital for safety, can also be frustrating, because being "tied" to a person essentially stops a dog's ability to act naturally. That being said, all dogs should be taught how to walk on the leash in a positive way without being jerked, yanked, choked, or shocked, so that walks can be enjoyable for everyone.

If you are overpowered by your dog's pulling and can't start teaching for fear of being pulled over, there are humane equipment solutions to help modify the pulling while you teach your dog to walk appropriately. A chest-led harness is a perfect training aid, as it takes pressure off a dog's sensitive neck area by distributing the pressure more evenly around the body. When the leash is attached to a ring located on the chest strap and your dog pulls, the harness will turn her body around rather than allowing her to go forward. I recommend this kind of harness for anyone who needs extra help, because safety must come first. Some dogs are so strong that they need a canine head collar, which acts the same way a halter does on a horse. Because the leash is attached to a metal loop located on the head collar under the dog's chin, the head automatically comes around when the dog pulls. I use head collars to help in severe cases, especially when clients are pregnant or elderly, but dogs need time to habituate to head collars as they can be uncomfortable at first. The owner must also be careful to prevent the dog from lunging forward; the dog's head can jerk around suddenly, potentially causing significant injury to her neck. Avoid the use of choke or prong collars, as these devices cause pain and significant physical damage to your dog's neck and spine.[1]

THE STOP AND BE STILL TECHNIQUE

Leash pulling is often successful for the dog because the person inadvertently reinforces the pulling by allowing the dog to go where she wants to when she pulls. But you can change this picture by changing the consequence for your dog. Whenever she pulls, immediately stop and stand completely still until the leash relaxes, either because your dog has taken a step back or has turned around to give you focus. When the leash is nicely relaxed, proceed on your walk. Repeat this as necessary.

THE REVERSE DIRECTION TECHNIQUE

If you find the preceding technique too slow, you can try the *reverse direction* method. When your dog pulls, issue a "let's go" cue, turn away from her, and walk off in the other direction without jerking on the leash. You can avoid yanking by motivating your dog to follow you with an excited voice to get her attention. When she is following you and the leash is relaxed, turn back and continue on your way. It may take a few turns, but your vocal cues and body language will make it clear that pulling will not be reinforced with forward movement, whereas walking calmly by your side or even slightly in front of you on a loose leash will allow your dog to get to where she wants to go. You can also reinforce your dog's decision to walk close to you by giving her a motivating reward when she is by your side.

VARY THE PICTURE

Once your dog is listening to you, you can vary the picture even more by becoming unpredictable yourself. This requires your dog to listen to you at all times, because she never knows when you might turn or where you are going to go next. Instead of turning away from her when you give the "let's go" cue, reverse direction by turning toward her. You can turn in a circle or do a figure eight. Any of these variations will get your dog's attention. Don't forget to praise her for complying, because the better you make her feel when she's walking close to you, the more she will choose to do so.

TEACHING THE "CLOSE" CUE

Walking well on a leash and walking right next to you are separate leash manner skills that your dog can learn.

As a dog's walking pace is naturally faster than a human's, be aware of how difficult it is for some dogs to modify their pace to suit yours. For some dogs, walking close to your side would be the same as if you were only allowed to walk down the street taking tiny baby steps—not easy or fun to do for long. Try starting this exercise beside a wall in your home so that your dog is between you and the wall. This makes it easier for her to stay close to your side.

- Teach your dog to follow a piece of food that you have in your hand. If your dog is not food motivated, use a toy instead.

- Show the food to your dog and then put it in your left or right hand. Hold your hand against the left or right side of your body, whichever is more comfortable so she learns to follow the food in your hand.

- Move forward and encourage her to follow the food, which now acts as a lure.

- Walk for about ten steps and then stop. Praise your dog and reward her with the food. If you want her to sit at this time, either give her the cue word or move closer into her body while saying "stop." That will teach her to stop and sit at the same time.

- Repeat this exercise several times, gradually increasing the number of steps you take.

Your goal is to show your dog that walking next to you brings her good things. The lure in your hand is the motivator and helps build up a hand signal that you can use with or without the "close" cue word.

- Repeat this technique until your dog is responding well. Say your dog's name followed by the cue "close" and move off with your hand tapping your side to encourage her to follow.

- Once you have compliance, begin using food intermittently while still praising her. If your dog goes in front of you, reverse direction and repeat the cue, tapping your thigh again. Praise her warmly.

- Vary the routine by turning left and right or doing a figure eight, saying "close" as you turn. The sit when you stop should now be automatic.

Make sure the close cue is well conditioned indoors before trying it out on the street. Don't expect your dog to walk right next to you all the time, but consider your dog's walking on a loose leash acceptable, with the close position available when you need it, reinforcing it for practice.

Eating Poop

My family and I were so excited to welcome our newest addition. We had found her at the shelter, curled up in a kennel run surrounded by other small dogs, wearing a pink "bunny girl" sweater with the words "Miss January" written on it. My intention was to rescue a dog that was sociable and outgoing, so naturally I fell for this fearful Chihuahua-Terrier mix curled up in the corner. Jasmine came into our lives, and we were relieved that with time and patience she blossomed into a quirky little pup that fell in love with us and her new canine buddy Sadie.

But because of her bad start in life, Jasmine had certain issues that had to be addressed, including one particularly unsavory habit: she loved to play with, sleep in, and eat poop. I discovered this one day while watching Sadie in the backyard and realized with horror that Jasmine was waiting behind Sadie's bottom as she toileted. As soon as the fresh, brown snack was accessible, Jasmine attacked it like a starved animal. I ran over, scooped her up and took her away from the offensive mess, but she was completely unfazed by my interruption, licking her lips to make sure she got every last delicious morsel.

As much as I explain to people that eating stool, though disgusting to us humans, is very normal in the dog world, I was horrified at the realization that *I* had a poop-eating dog. For a while I hoped that this had been an isolated incident, but unfortunately Jasmine proved me wrong. One bright fall morning while I was out of town filming *It's Me or the Dog*, my husband had put Jasmine in her crate for safety so that she couldn't walk around the house unsupervised while he took a shower. Coming out of the bathroom, he noticed a pungent smell, and with a quick inspection he saw that Jasmine had indeed pooped in her crate. As she was still new to us and not crate-trained (that is, trained not to toilet in the crate), my husband calmly cleaned up the mess and took her with him into his home office. She snuggled up on the chair next to him and all was peaceful until she began to gag. Fearing the worst, my husband cupped his hand under her chin as she vomited. Cursing quietly, he looked down at the mess to see what had made her throw up, and in the palm of his hand lay a nicely rounded ball of fresh stool. True to that earlier incident, Jasmine had eaten a decent portion of her most recent elimination.

Of course we humans find the thought of our dogs eating poop (called *coprophagia*) disgusting, but the unsavory fact is that some dogs find eating feces pleasurable. A dog may eat her own stool or that of another animal simply because she likes the taste. Cat poop is high on the list of tasty treats because of its high protein content and smell, but dogs consider deer and rabbit feces pretty scrumptious, too. Sadie and Jasmine love to hike with us in the mountains because there is always a feast of deer poop lying in wait for them.

Dogs that have a malabsorption disorder might not be able to easily extract the nutrients they need from the food, so stool becomes another chance to fulfill that nutritional need.[2] Other dogs eat feces because they're always hungry and enjoy getting two meals for the price of one. Simply feeding your dog a higher-quality food as well as dividing the food into multiple smaller meals throughout the day may satisfy the dog's hunger and quell the need to indulge elsewhere.

Although coprophagia is sometimes the result of a variety of medical conditions—including pancreatitis, intestinal infection, or food allergies—most cases are behavioral in nature. A new mother will stimulate her puppies to urinate and defecate by licking the anogenital area and will ingest the feces to keep the den clean. This makes the sleeping environment healthier for the pups and less detectable to predators. Because coprophagia can be a learned behavior, pups sometimes mimic their mother, in which case the action becomes a habit and is particularly hard to stop. Some mothers continue to eat poop after their puppies have been weaned because they find it pleasurable. Adult dogs may learn to eat poop by seeing other dogs indulging in the practice or because of human reinforcement. I once worked with a dog that toileted in the house, picked it up, and ran out the door to bury it in the backyard. I later discovered that a history of punishment after toileting in the home had actually taught him to take his poop and hide the evidence for fear of being punished if he was caught again.

Whatever the cause, eating feces can be unhealthy, especially if the stool is from an animal with intestinal parasites or an infectious disease. That's why even though Jasmine seemed to only like eating Sadie's stool as well as her own, I wanted to nip this behavior in the bud.

Jasmine had had a difficult start in life. The people who dropped her off at the shelter in a cardboard box told the staff that she rarely left her crate because she toileted around their home. So in addition to her being poorly housetrained, I suspected that Jasmine's poop-eating habit was the result of boredom and lack of proper care. I find this is often the case with puppies and dogs that come from puppy mills and pet stores. These dogs grow up in relative social isolation with no comfort and nothing to entertain them throughout the day, so the only thing they find to play with is their own feces. I noticed that Jasmine liked to pick up her poop and play with it like a ball—something she must have done frequently during many long, lonely hours of confinement.

Providing her with activity toys was a simple solution to this part of the problem. I wouldn't have been surprised if Jasmine had never seen a toy before she came to live with us, but when I rolled a ball toward her she jumped on it with delight and gleefully chased it around the room. As soon as I introduced her to toys and allowed her the freedom to play, she lost interest in playing with her poop. Jasmine is an orally fixated dog, continually using her mouth to explore her world by barking, licking, mouthing, nibbling, and chewing. By giving her durable chew toys, all of her energy, frustration, and oral needs could be directed onto something more appropriate. I also noticed that my little dog was a natural scavenger and, like many such dogs, ate everything she could find. I harnessed her scavenging needs by hiding toys around the house and teaching her to go and find them—the canine equivalent of a treasure hunt.

I also suspected that Jasmine was eating her feces simply because she liked the taste. Even though a dog's taste capabilities might not be as sensitive as ours, sense of smell plays a huge role in stimulating hunger, so if something smells nice, chances are it's going to taste nice too. With this in mind, some people try to stop their dogs eating feces by putting something bitter on the poop so that the smell and taste become offensive. The trouble with this practice is that bitter tastes are detected only if they pass over the rear third of the tongue, where the "bitter" taste buds are located, and if a dog gulps down her food in one bite, the unpleasant taste won't even register. This is also true if the bitter food is dry. Sprinkling poop with pepper, pineapple, or mint works occasionally, but some dogs experience adverse reactions to these substances. Cophrophagic dogs tend to eat very fast during mealtimes, which is part of the scavenger's instinct to eat food quickly before someone else gets a share. If your dog is inhaling her food at mealtimes and choking in the process, this is easily rectified by using a contoured feeding bowl or feeding all her meals through activity toys instead.

The only really effective solution for a poop-eating dog is to be vigilant and remove the feces as soon as the dog has toileted to avoid any chance of ingestion. Being aware of both of my dogs' toileting habits and removing the stool immediately meant that Jasmine was never able to indulge in the unsavory practice. Because her life is much richer and her diet is so healthy, an unpleasant habit has thankfully become a thing of the past.

Mouthing

Libby Evans sat down on the sofa, rolled up her sleeves, and showed me her arms. They were covered in bruises, gashes, and pitted holes that looked like cigarettes had been extinguished on them. "He started mouthing when he was four months old," she said, "and has never stopped. We've tried everything we know of to stop him biting us, but now he's getting too big and too dangerous."

Before we could talk any further, a tall, skinny male yellow Labrador leapt over the baby gate and ran over to Libby, throwing himself onto her lap and covering her face with licks. As she pushed him off, he redirected his attention onto her arms and began to mouth them as if they had just become two fabulous chew toys. He was relentless and oblivious to her protests, stopping only when he spied me in the room. In one swift move he turned and bolted toward me, leapt onto my lap, and began showering me with licks. Quickly tiring of this activity, he then hurled himself onto the floor to play with a half-chewed bone.

At first it seemed that Harvey was just being overly rambunctious, but as I observed him further he seemed to be getting increasingly frustrated. Having finished with the toy, he flung himself toward Libby once again and jumped on her with a wicked look in his eye. The more she told him no, the more his roughness increased and the harder he mouthed her arms. In a desperate attempt to stop the assault Libby screamed at him. Harvey stopped mouthing, curled the top of his lip into a frightening snarl, and leapt at her in a fit of rage. Before any more damage could be done, I ran to the other side of the room and started waving a toy like a crazy woman. As Harvey charged at me, I threw the toy into the kitchen and shut the door behind him as he ran to retrieve it. Libby looked at me with tears in her eyes and collapsed onto the sofa. For her the game had finished once and for all. Harvey had just had his last chance.

Harvey had been a Mother's Day gift. Libby's husband had neglected to get his wife a present, so while he was in the mall with his sons on a desperate, last-minute mission to save face, he spied a funny-looking puppy in the window of a pet store. Feeling his heart melt and wanting to gain kudos with his wife (who was still mourning the loss of her late beloved Labrador), he asked to see the puppy. Even though he knew that getting a puppy was not a great idea, good judgment flew out the window, and he left the store holding a squirmy little bundle of energy in his arms.

From the beginning, Libby noticed that Harvey never made eye contact with the family and didn't seem to want or need cuddles or attention. He slept less than "normal" puppies and was always getting into trouble. He was difficult to toilet train and didn't listen to anyone. He was taken to training class but was too distracted to learn anything so was asked to leave. He hated his crate and at night didn't give the family a moment's peace. He chewed the sofa cushions and had now begun to lift his leg and mark everything inside the home. Harvey seemed to be oblivious to any punishment, however severe. The family began to resent their puppy, and Harvey spent longer and longer periods in his crate. He was nothing like their former Labrador, and Libby's husband now regretted his purchase.

Mouthing is very normal in young puppies and begins as soon as they learn to suckle, bringing them food and comfort. When puppy teeth start coming through around three weeks of age, puppies learn that biting too hard on their mother either earns a reprimand or means that the source of food and comfort gets up and walks away. They also learn that mouthing, nipping, or biting their littermates too hard during play stops the game. When a puppy goes into a human home, owners must continue to let the puppy know that mouthing on clothes and skin is unacceptable. People who play roughly with their young dogs are reinforcing mouthy behavior through this play and often make it worse. Sometimes rough play causes arousal or anger, and the mouthing turns into something much more serious.

When puppies are taken away from their mother and littermates too early, they don't learn to inhibit their bite. Puppies from pet stores, for example, typically have mouthing issues because they are taken away from their mothers too soon at the puppy mill and are raised in sterile environments just at the most crucial time for social development. If these pups don't learn how to use their mouths correctly, their play bite becomes very hard. A dog that mouths hard in play also has the capacity to use her mouth when frustrated and angry.

All puppies and dogs need clear, consistent feedback from their human families that mouthing is unacceptable so that lessons learned from their canine mothers will transition well to a human home. Some trainers like to teach their dogs that gentle mouthing is acceptable, but I've found that clients have a hard time defining what is "acceptable" and what is not. What might be a soft mouth on an adult's arm, for example, is completely unacceptable on a child or elderly person's body, and even dogs with soft mouths can apply harder pressure when aroused. If I am playing with a pup that mouths me, I immediately stop the game either by removing the toy we are playing with or by getting up and walking away. I then wait for about ten seconds and resume the game. If the mouthing starts again, I repeat the process until the puppy learns that mouthing me stops play. Some pups and older dogs may continue to nip as I walk away. In these cases I have another person hold a very loose leash and gently guide the dog away. I also like to supply pups with toys to chew on, both to relieve the pressure on their teething gums and to redirect their mouthing from humans to something more appropriate.

Harvey, however, had been harshly reprimanded so frequently for his behavior that he became unresponsive and disconnected from his family. This in turn angered his family, who couldn't understand why their dog never listened to them. Harvey received continual punishment for all the things he did wrong and no praise for the few things he managed to do right. He spent an average of six to eight hours each day in his crate while the couple went to work. They had hired a dog walker to walk him during the day, but those walks had recently been stopped due to liability issues. By the time the family got home in the late afternoon, Harvey was a ball of pent-up energy. He exploded from his crate when released and didn't relent until he was put to bed at night.

As I gained more information from each family member, the picture became clearer. Harvey wasn't a bad dog; he was a bored, unstimulated, and frustrated adolescent that had been given too little exercise, few boundaries, and very little positive experience in his short life. Instead of looking at how his upbringing was affecting his behavior, the couple had concluded that Harvey was to blame.

I see this scenario all too often: despite there being so much education available on where to get a puppy and how to raise it successfully, Harvey had been an impulse buy, which is often doomed to fail right from the start. All too often companion-animal impulse buys end up being given away. As long as the pet stores keep selling puppies, puppy mills keep producing them, and people keep buying them, the cycle will continue.

In the meantime, Harvey's mind was spinning out of control. He was unable to focus on any one thing for more than a few seconds and was in constant motion, unable to settle. The four walls of the house were closing in on him, and the backyard had long ago ceased to be an exciting place. What Harvey needed was a large field to run and play in, a family that had more time for him, long walks, and a breed-specific sport or activity at which he could excel. There was no doubt in my mind that he would make an exceptional working dog, but I doubted that the family would be able to give him what he needed.

The first step in my behavior modification plan was to increase Harvey's daily exercise and put him on a predictable schedule. He was to be walked for at least an hour every day, which would increase when he reached adulthood. During the week, Harvey would go to day care (which he loved) for three days and would be walked twice a day by the dog walker for the rest of the working week. I usually recommend a mixture of day care and dog walkers, as some dogs become too overwhelmed or overstimulated going to day care every day. The family would walk Harvey on the weekends on a chest-led harness that eliminated his pulling so that Libby and her husband could easily teach him to walk properly on a regular leash and collar. I made his crate a much more pleasant place to be so that Harvey would feel comfortable using it for a nap or chew time or to have space away from the family when he needed it. Harvey's day became more structured, with teaching, chew time on appropriate toys, play, and walks with the family.

Because Libby's two boys had also experienced Harvey's hard mouth, I wanted to give them a way to interact and play safely with him under their parents' supervision. I tied a soft toy to a long rope and attached the rope to the end of an extendable pole. The pole and the rope kept the toy away from the children's bodies as they whirled it around, ensuring they had no physical contact with Harvey as he chased the toy. Now they could play with him safely without threat of injury if play got too rough. The game could also only be played if Harvey abided by the rules: lying down and waiting until the kids gave him the release cue to chase—a great lesson in self-control.

The results of increased attention and activity were almost immediate. For the first time in his life, Harvey actually began to enjoy interaction with his human family, and they in turn learned how to praise him, which gave him confidence. He was still an energetic dog that required a lot of time and energy, but things were improving. At the end of the day, living with an out-of-control Labrador might make for an entertaining Hollywood movie, but as Libby and her family found out, the reality can be very different.

If a dog must expend more energy controlling her impulses, she will have less energy to perform tasks that teach her self-control, so bear this in mind and observe when your dog has had enough. Remember that it can take longer for problem behaviors to be extinguished in adolescent dogs than in adults because adolescents have a harder time inhibiting their responses. If you are sensitive to your dog's needs, you will be able to tailor the teaching for maximum effect. Whether your dog inhibits her behavior consciously or unconsciously, never forget to tell her when she is doing a good job, because your feedback will make all the difference.

In Conclusion

Building and maintaining a healthy, balanced relationship with your dog doesn't have to be a battle. Although the teaching process can occasionally be difficult in our "I want it NOW" culture, taking the time to truly understand where our dogs came from, how they learn, and what they need in order to succeed in our strange, domesticated world can lead to one of the most satisfying and enriching relationships life can provide. The concepts, protocols, and techniques in this book are designed to help all owners more effectively and successfully live up to their end of the bargain of being their dog's best friend, whether the dog is generally well-behaved and needs only minor guidance and adjustments or suffers from more significant, ingrained behavioral issues. When we welcome dogs into our lives, we are signing an unwritten social contract that affirms our responsibility not just to care for, feed, and walk them, but also to help give them all the tools they need to experience the fullest, most rewarding life experience possible. Achieving this is possible only if we harness the power of positive training and ignore the shortcuts and pitfalls of punishment and dominance concepts.

As you continue the never-ending journey of discovery and fulfillment that comes with building a positive relationship with your dog, remember to be patient, positive, and persistent. Good luck!

Resources

OFFICIAL VICTORIA STILWELL WEBSITE

www.positively.com

FIND A VICTORIA STILWELL–LICENSED DOG TRAINER

Victoria Stilwell Positively Dog Training (VSPDT) is a global network of world-class positive-reinforcement dog trainers personally evaluated, approved, and licensed by Victoria Stilwell. VSPDT's dual mission is to help its members' businesses grow while promoting positive training ideologies worldwide to create healthy, balanced relationships based on mutual trust, respect, and love instead of pain, fear, and intimidation.

To find a Victoria Stilwell–Licensed dog trainer visit www.positively.com/trainers.

TRAINING TOOLS AND PRODUCTS

Victoria recommends only the use of humane canine training tools and products. Due to the ever-changing nature of the pet product industry, Victoria regularly updates the products she uses and approves and makes them available on her website at www.positively.com/store.

TRAINING VIDEOS

Victoria provides dog training and informational videos on her various online platforms and in partnership with eHow at www.youtube.com/ehowpets.

CANINE NOISE PHOBIA SERIES

In partnership with Through a Dog's Ear, Victoria has developed the groundbreaking Canine Noise Phobia Series, a unique compilation of specialized audio recordings and innovative training protocols specifically designed to reduce and prevent noise phobias and anxiety in dogs. Available treatments include: Thunderstorms, Fireworks, City Sounds, and Calming. Find out more at www.caninenoisephobia.com. Available at www.positively.com/store.

RESCUE AND ANIMAL WELFARE ORGANIZATIONS

American Humane Association: Since 1877, the American Humane Association has been a global leader committed to protecting children, pets, and farm animals from abuse and neglect. www.americanhumane.org

RedRover: Founded in 1987, RedRover focuses on bringing animals out of crisis and strengthening the bond between people and animals through a variety of programs, including emergency sheltering, disaster relief services, financial assistance, and education. www.redrover.org

CANINE ASSISTANTS

A leading nonprofit organization, Canine Assistants trains and provides service dogs for children and adults with physical disabilities or other special needs. www.canineassistants.org

VICTORIA STILWELL FOUNDATION

The Victoria Stilwell Foundation (VSF) is a national 501(c)3 charitable foundation, the mission of which is to support assistance dog organizations and smaller rescue shelters while promoting Victoria Stilwell's core positive reinforcement dog training philosophies. Founded in 2009, VSF's primary purpose is to provide financial assistance and canine behavior expertise to organizations devoted to bettering the lives of both dogs and humans.
www.positively.com/foundation
Donate to VSF: www.positively.com/donate

RECOMMENDED READING

- *Aggressive Behavior in Dogs*, James O'Heare
- *Animals in Translation*, Temple Grandin and Catherine Johnson
- *Before and After Getting Your Puppy: The Positive Approach to Raising a Happy, Healthy, and Well-Behaved Dog*, Ian Dunbar
- *Bones Would Rain from the Sky: Deepening Our Relationships with Dogs*, Suzanne Clothier
- *The Culture Clash: A Revolutionary New Way of Understanding the Relationship Between Humans and Domestic Dogs*, Jean Donaldson
- *Dog Sense: How the New Science of Dog Behavior Can Make You a Better Friend to Your Pet*, John Bradshaw
- *Don't Leave Me! Step-by-Step Help for Your Dog's Separation Anxiety*, Nicole Wilde
- *Don't Shoot the Dog! The New Art of Teaching and Training*, Karen Pryor
- *For the Love of a Dog*, Patricia B. McConnell
- *Handbook of Applied Dog Behavior and Training, Vol. 1: Adaptation and Learning*, Steven R. Lindsay and Victoria Lea Voith

- *Handbook of Applied Dog Behavior and Training, Vol. 2: Etiology and Assessment of Behavior Problems,* Steven R. Lindsay
- *Handbook of Applied Dog Behavior and Training, Vol. 3: Procedures and Protocols,* Steven R. Lindsay
- *Help for Your Fearful Dog: A Step-by-Step Guide to Helping Your Dog Conquer His Fears,* Nicole Wilde
- *How Dogs Think: What the World Looks Like to Them and Why They Act the Way They Do,* Stanley Coren
- *How to Speak Dog: Mastering the Art of Dog-Human Communication,* Stanley Coren
- *Inside of a Dog: What Dogs See, Smell, and Know,* Alexandra Horowitz
- *It's Me or the Dog: How to Have the Perfect Pet,* Victoria Stilwell
- *On Talking Terms with Dogs: Calming Signals,* Turid Rugaas
- *The Other End of the Leash: Why We Do What We Do Around Dogs,* Patricia B. McConnell
- *Perfect Puppy in 7 Days: How to Start Your Puppy Off Right,* Sophia Yin
- *The Power of Positive Dog Training,* Pat Miller
- *Reaching the Animal Mind: Clicker Training and What It Teaches Us About All Animals,* Karen Pryor
- *The Thinking Dog,* Gail Fisher
- *Through a Dog's Ear: Using Sound to Improve the Health and Behavior of Your Canine Companion,* Joshua Leeds and Susan Wagner
- *Through a Dog's Eyes: Understanding Our Dogs by Understanding How They See the World,* Jennifer Arnold
- *The Well-Adjusted Dog: Dr. Dodman's 7 Steps to Lifelong Health and Happiness for Your Best Friend,* Nicholas Dodman

Endnotes

CHAPTER 1. DOMINANCE AND PACK THEORY

1. Geoffrey John Syme, "Experimental Investigations of Social Behaviour in Animals: Competitive Orders as Measures of Social Dominance" (PhD diss., University of Canterbury, 2007), http://hdl.handle.net/10092/4923.

2. Roberto Bonanni, Paula Valsecchi, and Eugenia Natoli, "Pattern of Individual Participation and Cheating in Conflicts Between Groups of Free-ranging Dogs," *Animal Behavior* 79 (2010), doi:10.1016/j.anbehav.2010.01.016.

3. John Bradshaw and Helen Nott, "Social and Communication Behavior in Companion Dogs," in *The Domestic Dog, Its Evolution, Behavior and Interactions with People,* ed. James Serpell (Cambridge: Cambridge University Press, 1996), 116–17.

4. Erik Zimen, "On the Regulation of Pack Size in Wolves," *Zeitschrift für Tierpsychologie* 40 (1976).

5. David Mech, *The Wolf: Ecology and Behavior of an Endangered Species* (New York: Natural History Press, 1970); "Wolf News and Info," Dave Mech, http://www.davemech.org/news .html; Fred H. Harrington and Paul C. Paquet, eds.,*Wolves of the World: Perspectives of Behavior, Ecology, and Conservation* (Park Ridge, New Jersey: Noyes Publications, 1982).

6. Márta Gácsi et al., "Species-specific Differences and Similarities in the Behavior of Hand-raised Dog and Wolf Pups in Social Situations with Humans," *Developmental Psychobiology* 47, no. 2 (2005): 111–22.

7. Ibid.

8. "Smarter Than You Think: Renowned Canine Researcher Puts Dogs' Intelligence on Par with 2-Year-Old Human," American Psychological Association, last modified August 8, 2009. http://www.apa.org/news/press/ releases/2009/08/dogs-think.aspx[2].

9. Meghan Herron et al., "Survey of the Use and Outcome of Confrontational and Non-Confrontational Methods in Client-Owned Dogs Showing Undesired Behaviors," *Journal of Applied Animal Behaviour Science* 117, no. 1–2 (2009): 47–54, doi:10.1016/j.applanim.2008.12.011.

10. Bonne Beerda et al., "Behavioural, Saliva Cortisol and Heart Rate Responses to Different Types of Stimuli in Dogs," *Applied Animal Behaviour Science* 58, no. 3–4 (1998): 365–81, doi:10.1016/S0168-1591(97)00145-7.

CHAPTER 2. THE POWER OF POSITIVE TRAINING

1. E. F. Hiby, N. J. Rooney, and J. W. S. Bradshaw, "Dog Training Methods: Their Use, Effectiveness and Interaction with Behaviour and Welfare," *Animal Welfare* 13 (2004): 63–69.

2. R. J. Herrnstein, "On the Law of Effect," *Journal of the Experimental Analysis of Behavior* 13, no. 2 (1970): 243–66.

3. Temple Grandin and Catherine Johnson, *Animals in Translation* (New York: Harcourt Books, 2005).

CHAPTER 3. LEADING WITHOUT FORCE

1. Paula Bloom, clinical psychologist: www.paulabloom.com.

2. Paula Bloom, interview by Victoria Stilwell and Holly Firfer, *Positively Podcast*, Episode 208, December 2, 2011, http://positively.com/2011/12/02/positively-podcast-episode-208.

3. "Position Statement on the Use of Dominance Theory in Behavior Modification in Animals," American Veterinary Society of Animal Behavior, 2008. http://avsabonline.org/uploads/position_statements/dominance_statement.pdf.

4. David Mech, "Whatever Happened to the Term Alpha Wolf?" *International Wolf* 18, no. 4 (2008): 7, http://www.wolf.org/wolves/news/pdf/winter2008.pdf.

CHAPTER 4. BUILDING THE BOND

1. Kerstin Uvnas-Moberg, "Role of Oxytocin in Human Animal Interaction," in *People and Animals—For Life. 12th International Association of Human-Animal Interaction Organizations Conference, Abstract Book* (Stockholm, Sweden: 2010), 7, http://iahaio.org/files/conference2010stockholm.pdf.

2. Miho Nagasawa et al., "Dogs' Gaze at Its Owner Increases Owner's Urinary Oxytocin During Social Interaction, "*Hormones and Behavior* 55, no. 3 (2008): 434–41, doi: 10.1016/j.yhbeh.2008.12.002.

3. Kerstin Uvnas-Moberg and M. Petersson, "Oxytocin, a Mediator of Anti-Stress, Well Being, Social Interaction, Growth and Healing," *Z Psychosom Med Psychother* 51, no. 1 (2005): 57–80.

4. Kun Guo et al., "Left Gaze Bias in Humans, Rhesus Monkeys and Domestic Dogs," *Animal Cognition* 12, no. 3 (2008): 1–28.

5. Timothy Condon and Glenn Elert, "Frequency Range of Dog Hearing," *The Physics Factbook*, http://hypertextbook.com/facts/2003/TimCondon.shtml.

6. Joshua Leeds and Susan Wagner, *Through a Dog's Ear: Using Sound to Improve the Health and Behavior of Your Canine Companion* (Boulder, CO: Sounds True, 2008).

7. Alexandra Horowitz, *Inside of a Dog: What Dogs See, Smell, and Know* (New York: Simon and Schuster, 2009).

8. Stanley Coren, *How Dogs Think: Understanding the Canine Mind* (New York: Free Press, 2004).

9. J. C. Dennis et al., "Immunohistochemistry of the Canine Vomeronasal Organ," *Journal of Anatomy* 202, no. 6 (2003): 329–38, doi: http://dx.crossref.org/10.1046%2Fj.1469-7580.2003.00190.x; D. R. Adams and M. D. Wiekamp, "The Canine Vomeronasal Organ," *Journal of Anatomy* 138 no. 4 (1984): 771–87.

10. Young-Mee Kim et al., "Efficacy of Dog-Appeasing Pheromone (DAP) for Ameliorating Separation-Related Behavioral Signs in Hospitalized Dogs," *The Canadian Veterinary Journal* 51, no. 4 (2010): 380–84.

11. Coren, *How Dogs Think*.

12. Ibid.

13. "What Is T-Touch?" Linda Tellington-Jones, 2012, http://www.ttouch.com/whyTTouch.shtml.

14. *Dictionary.com*, s.v. "jealousy," http://dictionary.reference
.com/browse/jealousy?

15. John Bradshaw, *Dog Sense: How the New Science of Dog Behavior Can Make You a Better Friend to Your Pet* (New York: Basic Books, 2011), 213–18.

16. Horowitz, *Inside of a Dog*.

17. J. David Smith, "Inaugurating the Study of Animal Metacognition," *International Journal of Comparative Psychology* 23 (2010): 401–13.

18. S. McMahon, K. MacPherson, and W. A. Roberts, "Dogs Choose a Human Informant: Metacognition in Canines," *Behavioural Processes* 85(3): 293–98.

CHAPTER 5. THE POSITIVE PUPPY

1. "Purdue University's Recommendations for Puppy Classes," Andrew Luesher and Steve Thompson, http://www
.mannersformutts.com/puppies/purdue_university.html.

2. Coren, *How Dogs Think*.

CHAPTER 7. HOME-ALONE BLUES

1. Joshua Leeds and Susan Wagner, *Through a Dog's Ear*.

2. "Facts—Pet Ownership," American Humane Association, http://www.petfinder.com/for-shelters/facts-pet-ownership.html.

3. Nicholas Dodman, *The Well-Adjusted Dog: Dr. Dodman's 7 Steps to Lifelong Health and Happiness for Your Best Friend* (New York: Houghton Mifflin Harcourt, 2008).

CHAPTER 8. STRESS, ANXIETY, AND FEAR

1. Franklin McMillan and Kathryn Lance, *Unlocking the Animal Mind: How Your Pet's Feelings Hold the Key to His Health and Happiness* (Emmaus, PA: Rodale Books, 2004).

2. Steven R. Lindsay, *Handbook of Applied Dog Behavior and Training, Vol. 3: Procedures and Protocols* (Oxford: Wiley-Blackwell, 2005), 5.

3. M. Mendl, "Performing Under Pressure: Stress and Cognitive Function," *Applied Animal Behaviour Science* 65, no. 3 (1999): 221–44.

4. E. A. Shull-Selcer and W. Stagg, "Advances in the Understanding and Treatment of Noise Phobias," *Veterinary Clinics of North America: Small Animal Practice* 21 (1991): 353–67; Steven R. Lindsay, *Handbook of Applied Dog Behavior and Training, Vol. 3.,* 158.

5. Nicholas Dodman, *Dogs Behaving Badly: An A-Z Guide to Understanding and Curing Behavioral Problems in Dogs* (New York: Bantam Books, 1999), 67–71.

6. "Obsessive-Compulsive Disorder (OCD)," Mayo Foundation for Medical Education and Research, last modified Dec. 15, 2010, www.mayoclinic.com/health/obsessive-compulsive-disorder/DS00189.

7. "Syringomyelia (SM) and the Cavalier King Charles Spaniel," CavalierHealth.org, http://cavalierhealth.org/syringomyelia.htm; Capello et al. (2006) *International Conference on Syringomyelia.* Royal Veterinary College, London.

8. H. D. Pederson et al., "Idiopathic Asymptomatic Thrombocytopenia in Cavalier King Charles Spaniels Is an Autosomal Recessive Trait," *Journal of Veterinary Internal Medicine* 16, no. 2 (2002): 169–73.

9. Dodman, *The Well-Adjusted Dog,* 170–73.

CHAPTER 9. CANINE AGGRESSION

1. O'Heare, *Aggressive Behavior in Dogs*.

2. Katherine Simpson, "The Role of Testosterone in Aggression," *McGill Journal of Medicine* 6 (2001): 32–40; J. C. Neilson et al., "Effects of Castration on Problem Behaviors in Male Dogs with Reference to Age and Duration of Behavior," *Journal of the American Veterinary Medical Association* 211, no. 2 (1997): 180–82.

3. D. S. Caldwell and P. B. Little, "Aggression in Dogs and Associated Neuropathology," *The Canadian Veterinary Journal* 21, no. 5 (1980): 152–54.

4. Steven Hamilton and Karen Overall, "Canine Behavioral Genetics Project" (ongoing research, University of California, San Francisco), http://psych.ucsf.edu/clinical-trials .aspx?id=1280

5. Matthijs B. H. Shilder and Joanne A. M. Van der Borg, "Training Dogs with Help of the Shock Collar: Short and Long Term Behavioural Effects," *Applied Animal Behavior Science* 85 (2004): 319–34; R. H. Polsky, "Electronic Shock Collars: Are They Worth the Risk?," *Journal of the American Animal Hospital Association* 30, no. 5 (1994):463–68; Emily Blackwell and Rachel Casey, "The Use of Shock Collars and Their Impact on the Welfare of Dogs," *Royal Society for the Prevention of Cruelty to Animals* (2006), http://www.rspca .org.uk/ImageLocator/LocateAsset?asset=document&asse tId=1232713013325&mode=prd.

6. J. Sacks et al., "Breeds of Dogs Involved in Fatal Human Attacks in the United States Between 1979 and 1988," *Journal of the American Veterinary Medical Association* 217 (2000): 836–40.

7. John Denko, "The Public Safety and Humane Implications of Persistently Tethering Domestic Dogs" (Report to the Consumer and Public Affairs Committee, January 10, 2008, New Mexico Department of Public Safety), http://www .apnm.org/campaigns/chaining/Final_DPS_Tethering_ Study.pdf.

8. R. H. Polsky, "Can Aggression in Dogs Be Elicited Through the Use of Electronic Pet Containment Systems?" *Journal of Applied Animal Welfare Science 3*, no. 4 (2000): 345–57.

9. "Hospital Admissions Caused by Dogs on the Rise," The Information Centre, NHS, http://www.ic.nhs.uk/ news-and-events/news/hospital-admissions-caused-by -dogs-on-the-rise-say-provisional-figures-which-highlight -seasonal-and-regional-patterns.

10. US Department of Health & Human Services, Agency for Healthcare Research and Quality, "Hospital Admissions for Dog Bites Increase 86 Percent Over a 16-Year Period," *AHRQ News and Numbers*, December 6, 2010, http://www .ahrq.gov/news/nn/nn120110.htm.

11. "Dog Bite: Fact Sheet," Centers for Disease Control and Pre-vention, last modified April 1, 2008, http://www.cdc.gov/ HomeandRecreationalSafety/Dog-Bites/dogbite-factsheet .html.

12. H. E. Nasser and P. Overberg, "Census Reveals Plummeting U.S. Birthrates," *USA Today*, June 2, 2011, http://www .usatoday.com/news/nation/census/2011-06-03-fewer -children-census-suburbs_n.htm.

13. Jim Crosby, "2007—Fatal Attack Facts and Figures," *Canine Aggression Issues with Jim Crosby* (blog), January 20, 2008, http://canineaggression.blogspot.com/2008/01/2007-fatal -attack-facts-and-figures.html.

14. "Dog Bites," American Humane Association, http://www
    .americanhumane.org/animals/stop-animal-abuse/fact
    -sheets/dog-bites.html.

15. Ilana R. Reisner, Frances S. Shofer, and Michael L. Nance,
    "Behavioral Assessment of Child-Directed Canine Aggres-
    sion," *Injury Prevention* 13, no. 5 (2007): 348–51.

CHAPTER 10. SOLVING COMMON BEHAVIOR PROBLEMS

1. Anders Hallgren, *Animal Behavior Consultants Newsletter* 9,
   no. 3 (1992).

2. L. Freeman et al., "WSAVA Nutritional Assessment Guidelines," *Journal of Small Animal Practice* 52, no. 7 (2011):
   385–96.

About the Author

Born and raised in Wimbledon, England, VICTORIA STILWELL is one of the world's most recognized and respected dog trainers. She is best known for her role as the star of her hit TV series *It's Me or the Dog* through which she is able to share her insight and passion for positive reinforcement dog training, and as a judge on CBS's *Greatest American Dog*. Having filmed over one hundred episodes since 2005, Stilwell reaches audiences in over fifty countries while counseling families on their pet problems.

In the early 1990s, Stilwell began her career in pet training when she created her own successful dog-walking company
and immediately recognized the need for qualified professionals
to help her clients with the training process. While pursuing a
successful acting career (working in London's West End as well
as in numerous films, TV series, commercials, and voiceovers),
she expanded her focus to dog training by learning from some of
Britain's most respected positive reinforcement dog trainers and
behaviorists.

After moving to the United States with her husband, Stilwell cofounded several successful dog training companies up and
down the East Coast, quickly establishing herself as one of New
York's most sought-after dog trainers. With a particular fondness
for rescue animals in need of behavior rehabilitation, Stilwell
devoted much of her time and energy to a number of animal rescue organizations in New York and Atlanta, serving as a behavior
advisor and giving regular seminars on the subject of dog rescue,
training, and rehabilitation while becoming one of the leading
voices in the field of dog training and behavior.

A passionate advocate for positive reinforcement dog training
methods, Stilwell is the editor in chief of Positively.com, which
features the world's leading veterinary behaviorists, dog trainers,
and behavioral scientists on her Positively Expert Blog. She is a
vocal opponent of punitive, dominance-based training techniques
that often result in "quick fixes" but ultimately cause more long-
term harm than good while damaging the owner-dog relationship. Her first two best-selling books, *It's Me or the Dog: How to
Have the Perfect Pet* and *Fat Dog Slim: How to Have a Healthy, Happy
Pet*, have been widely praised.

A regular guest on talk shows, news broadcasts, and radio
programs in the United States, Europe, and Asia, Stilwell was
named 2009's Dog Trainer of the Year at the Purina ProPlan Dog

awards and was the recipient of the prestigious 2011 Excellence in Journalism and Outstanding Contributions to the Pet Industry Award. *It's Me or the Dog* has been the recipient of multiple honors including 2011 and 2012 Genesis Award Nominations and a 2009 People's Choice Award nomination. Stilwell is a regular columnist for several magazines and has been featured in numerous journals, magazines, and newspapers including the *New York Times, USA Today, Cosmopolitan, Time.com, Oprah, Rachael Ray Everyday, MSNBC.com, Self, Shape,* the *Daily Mail,* and the *Sun.*

Stilwell is the CEO of Victoria Stilwell Positively Dog Training—the world's premier global network of positive reinforcement dog trainers. In addition to her globally available Positively Podcast series, she also produces several shows in her role as the director of training and behavior for the popular eHow Pets YouTube channel.

Stilwell is committed to helping the cause of animal rescue and rehabilitation and is heavily involved with organizations around the world to increase awareness of puppy mills, dog fighting, animal abuse, pet overpopulation, dog bite prevention, and other animal-related causes. A cofounder of the national Dog Bite Prevention conference series, Stilwell is also a National Ambassador for the American Humane Association and serves on the advisory boards of both RedRover and DogTV. She is a member of several professional dog training associations.

Victoria currently resides in Atlanta with her husband, Van, daughter, Alex, and two rescue dogs, Sadie and Jasmine.

Index

Index